Deprived of Unhappiness

Also by Sam Pickering

BOOKS OF ESSAYS

A Continuing Education
The Right Distance
May Days
Still Life
Let It Ride
Trespassing
Walkabout Year
The Blue Caterpillar
Living to Prowl

LITERARY STUDIES

The Moral Tradition in English Fiction, 1785–1850
John Locke and Children's Books in Eighteenth-Century England
Moral Instruction and Fiction for Children, 1749–1820

Deprived of Unhappiness

Sam Pickering

OHIO UNIVERSITY PRESS

ATHENS

Ohio University Press, Athens, Ohio 45701
© 1998 by Sam Pickering
Printed in the United States of America
All rights reserved

Ohio University Press books are printed on acid-free paper ⊗ ™

03 02 01 00 99 98   5 4 3 2 1

Book design by Chiquita Babb

Library of Congress Cataloging-in-Publication Data
Pickering, Samuel, F., 1941–
    Deprived of unhappiness / Sam Pickering.
    p.   cm.
    ISBN 0-8214-1234-5 (cloth : alk. paper)
    I. Title.
    AC8.P662 1998
814.'54—dc21   98-24080
                                                CIP

For Vicki:

"A perfect Woman, nobly planned,
To warn, to comfort, and command;
And yet a Spirit still, and bright
With something of angelic light."

Contents

Preface

$\mathcal{T}$his summer classes ended at the middle school on June 16. "Daddy," Eliza asked at dinner that night, "what will we do tomorrow?" "The real question," Vicki responded, "is 'what will tomorrow do to us?' " Essayists, Montaigne once explained, portray passing. For an essayist anything can furnish a sentence, not only things done by or to a person but things that swirl around, or more likely bounce lazily along. Early the next morning I drank coffee and ate a muffin at the Cup of Sun. "I'm a bit dopey," my friend Pam said. "Instead of taking my medicine at breakfast, I swallowed the dog's pills." Suddenly the day seemed full, and I eavesdropped on imaginary conversations. "How is Pam?" I heard Ellen ask. "Aside from an inordinate interest in telephone poles, she seems in fine fettle," Roger replied. "What's the matter with Pam?" Lee asked after meeting her on the sidewalk. "I said 'good morning' to her, and she almost bit my head off." Later I heard that Pam so disgraced herself in aerobics class that the instructor asked her to withdraw from the course. Modesty forbids describing Pam's misbehavior in detail. The instructor did say, though, that if Pam successfully negotiated the heel and fetch of obedience school, she could re-enroll.

What might be said leads to what is said. Pam's medication affected me more than her. After finishing the muffin, I trotted across campus, words yapping through my mind. Near the bookstore I met the new dean of arts and sciences. In hopes of leashing matters academic, the dean tightened chains binding two departments and slapped a flea collar on another, in the process causing much growling and gnashing of teeth. "I'm sorry to hear that the president has been forced to assign you a bodyguard," I said, leaning forward, almost as if I were pointing a covey of quail.

In contrast to the moralist who sees clearly and damns the half-truth as a whole lie, the essayist pencils paths through hazy landscapes. Although I live and write simply, I prefer bright lies to drab truths. As a result some of my lines go crooked. Occasionally the straying bothers a reader. "If you want to be known for literary high seriousness," a critic wrote me, "you should tell the truth." Alas, essayists are low, not elevated, flyers. Rarely does an essayist imagine that the sparrow he hatched is an eagle.

For me tomorrow rarely creeps forward at a dull, uneventful pace. After flushing surprise from the dean's face, I ambled home. Mail had arrived. One of mother's bridesmaids sent me a clipping from the *Richmond Times-Dispatch*. Ratcliffe Florist, founded by my grandfather and which, the paper noted, "had operated in downtown Richmond since 1911," had closed, its customer list being taken over by Strange's Florist. For a moment I pondered time's passing. Grandfather died in 1948 and Mother in 1988. The last time I was in Richmond the town had changed so much that I felt lost. *"Strange, estranged,"* I muttered, toying with words, "how fitting that a florist named Strange should buy the list." Rather than hardheaded, essayists are softhearted. When the pond in his backyard dried up, one essayist greased cracks in the mud with Crisco, or so the dean told me. Because days and people are various, essayists don't reduce life to certainty. Just as I started to think about the clipping, Doug the plumber arrived to connect the ice-maker in the refrigerator. The next day Doug was leaving for vacation in North Carolina. Doug ran the air conditioner in his bedroom all year, even during winter. He'd become so accustomed to the rumble that he couldn't sleep in a quiet room. Consequently he recorded the sound of the air conditioner. Whenever he left Storrs, he packed the tape and played it at night, no matter that the rooms in which he stayed were air conditioned.

Tight shoes, as the saying puts it, pave dirt roads. Not wanting to blister days with purpose, essayists go barefoot. That night on the radio Vicki heard a preacher confess that he "sometimes felt like flat pop—a whole lot of liquid, not a lot of fizz." The carbonation, he declared, "goes out of my life." "Soda for the soul," Vicki said, "what a world!" Religious stories bubble through my essays. The stories appear because I enjoy biblical event and language, not because I want to eradicate either vice, or virtue. According to a Coptic story, when Christ was a child, He traveled with Mary and Joseph from Nazareth to Acre. During the trip He spent an afternoon playing in the sand dunes under the shadow of Mt. Carmel. Instead of a castle or a sea monster He sculpted birds. At dusk when Mary called Him to dinner, He leaped to his feet and clapped His hands, whereupon the sculptures turned into real birds, and bursting from the earth soared toward Jerusalem. According to one account the sculptures became great white egrets. In another version of the tale they turned into a mixed flock of white storks and great crested grebes.

Tongues shred stories faster than feet wear holes in rugs. Old stories resemble quilts, different ages patching squares of prose over original fabrics. In a more recent version of the story Time has transformed the crested grebe into the little grebe or dabchick, an emblem, a commentator explained, "of the poor and the meek celebrated in the beatitudes." In literary matters, as in daily life, it pays to pester. The story interested me, and I plucked at the stitching until I uncovered forgotten bits of narrative. The sea eagle, I discovered, once sang more sweetly than the lyre. Indeed, according to a story told on Rhodes, the sirens were actually sea eagles. That musical history aside, however, in a revision of the Coptic tale the sea eagle killed one of the birds sculpted by Christ. Eating the bird burned the eagle's throat. Afterward when the eagle tried to sing, his cries resembled barking. Definitive versions of old tales rarely exist. Just as I folded the story to place it in a sugar chest of the mind, I stumbled upon a version that transformed the eagle into a honey buzzard. Because he killed one of Christ's birds, the buzzard was condemned to raid the nests of bees and wasps, in the process being stung by both insects and remorse.

Much as I didn't dog Pam in order to study the effects of the pills, so I don't always unravel story. According to Macedonian tale, rats bred so rapidly on Noah's ark that they threatened to strip the granaries and starve the other animals. Taking pity upon the ruminating generations, the Lord told Noah to massage the spine of the female tiger. Noah followed the Lord's instructions. Shortly afterward the tiger gave birth to a pair of cats. Within a week all rats except a single reclusive pair had vanished. Jealous of her husband, Noah's wife decided to go him one better, and she rubbed the back of the female hippopotamus. The hippopotamus gave birth to two pigs. The pigs soiled the ark badly. They overturned garbage bins and so scattered trash that when the floodwaters abated Noah burned the ark so that it would not pollute the land, thus becoming the world's first ecologist. Even worse, the pigs gnawed a head off the two-headed snake. Since one of its heads was male and the other female, the serpent had never wasted hours trying to please a mate and as a result was the kindest, most temperate creature on the ark. Losing a head, however, poisoned the snake's character. Forced to crawl through dirt looking for a mate made the snake so bitter it became venomous.

I often uncover fragments of story. Last week in an old religious catalogue I discovered posters depicting the Tree of Everlasting Life and its companion the Tree of Eternal Damnation. Both trees resembled rosebushes. On the Tree of Everlasting Life, faces of the sanctified bloomed, singing "gladsome lays of Immanuel's love." Over their cheeks petals tumbled soft as dew. In contrast, on the Tree of Eternal Damnation the heads of the doomed blew shortly after budding, black hornets with skulls for faces buzzing around them, stinging incessantly. From limbs of the tree, thorns jutted sharp as knives. When the furnaces of Hell expelled hot winds, the limbs snapped back and forth and the thorns sliced the faces of the damned. "When storms rage in your world," the catalogue warned, "the sounds you hear are not winds but the unsanctified moaning and howling."

Much as cats purr to please themselves, essayists are willful, writing about matters that entertain them. Although I roam family and town, I also spend hours writing in my study. Like the birds sculpted by Jesus, the tales I sketch sometimes, to me at least, seem as real as matters domestic or academic. Although no one else is in the study when I write, rarely am I alone. A host of fictional characters clamors through paragraphs, enlivening my present. Home to three generations of my family, Carthage, Tennessee, is an actual town. In my essays, however, the real Carthage is a shadow behind a fiction.

Otha Hogletree was a sometime lumberman and a full-time ne'er-do-well. Otha blamed his failures upon luck, explaining that he was born when the Cumberland River was low. "People born when rivers are high are always fortunate," he explained in Ankerrow's Café one afternoon. "Folks birthed at low waters are doomed to misfortune and suffering." In truth, Otha was shiftless and parsimonious, and character, not luck, was responsible for his lack of success. "Otha would skin an ant for tallow," Loppie Groat said. According to Turlow Gutheridge, Otha was so tight he squeaked when he walked. Otha once tried to raise sheep. He failed, Turlow said, because he was lazy. When thistles took over his pasture, he did not dig them out, calling them "labor-saving devices." "When sheep brush against the burrs, hooks will snag their wool and shear them, saving me a heap of work." Otha also drank, and most days his skin was yellow as a pumpkin. One morning after a long night's drinking, he stumbled into Ankerrow's Café, saying that a black dog with the head of a woman had chased him through town, disappearing only when he reached the Gainesboro crossroads. "Then," he said, "the dog exploded just like it had dropsy, spraying water all over me." By afternoon, story transformed the dog into a headless calf with a knothole for a neck, from which a woodpecker, sticking its bill out, stabbed Otha in the bottom. Because of the drinking, Otha's wife Meleeta left him, saying she couldn't wait to dance on his grave. After hearing Meleeta's remark, Otha instructed Slubey Garts, owner of the Haskins Funeral Home, to bury him in Dunphy's Pond.

One night after a day of carousing at Enos Mayfield's Inn in South Carthage, Otha knocked a bottle of ink into the chamberpot by his bed. Otha was so tight he didn't realize what he'd done. The ink stained the contents of the pot black, and the next morning, when Otha dumped the pot out the kitchen window, he noticed the color. Thinking he was dying, he went back to bed. A member of the Crystal Fountain Rebekah Lodge for thirty years, Meleeta visited Otha. "Meleeta," Otha said, "I know I treated you poorly, but after I'm gone, I want you to open the door and the window to this bedroom so angels won't have no hindrance taking my soul." "Leave the room open!" Meleeta told Turlow Gutheridge later; "I don't reckon angels will be fetching Otha's soul. He'd be well advised to lock the door and bolt the window." Because Otha was a regular patron of the Inn, Enos bought him a pint of whiskey as a going-away present. Inspired by drink, Otha did the only decent thing, as Turlow put it, that he ever did in his life. After finishing the pint, Otha sloshed gasoline around the bedroom and burned himself up, reducing the house to ashes so that his sons Skeets and Mitch would not have an inheritance over which to quarrel.

When a dollar walks into a room, dimes aren't so attractive. If dollars are epics and dimes lyrics, and if a novel by Dickens is worth sixty-five cents and one by Faulkner forty or so, my essays are worth a nickel on the literary cash register. The weathered stories I tell about Carthage spot my essays and reduce their value. Still, I prefer the rumpled to the starched. Just yesterday Turlow sent me a letter stained with news. So that he would appear more professional, Dr. Sollows bought a skull and the bones of a right hand for his office. There having been a profitable rash of stabbings in Nashville, the medical school at Vanderbilt enjoyed a surplus of parts, which the dean offered to alumni at bargain, or as the advertisement put it, at "skeletal prices." Dr. Sollows assumed the bones would arrive in a box of wood shavings. Unfortunately they arrived in dry ice with the meat still attached. Printed on a strip of paper pasted to the skull were instructions for boiling the flesh away. Meleeta cooked meals at the Walton Hotel. A bachelor, Dr. Sollows ate at the hotel and knew that Meleeta owned a copper kettle. Explaining that he had to do some cooking, Dr. Sollows borrowed the kettle and boiled the skull and hand down to bones. Only later did Meleeta discover how the doctor had used her kettle. "And to tell the truth," she told Turlow, "I just haven't felt the same about cooking greens in that kettle. Every time I throw in the hog jowl I get the all-over shivers."

Life sprawls. Dog pills, theological soda pop, turnip greens seasoned with honey buzzard—essayists are hearty, flexible trenchermen. When plans or paragraphs fail, the essayist moves on to something else, though I should add that essayists don't adapt to circumstance quite so smoothly as the vulture who told his wife that her giving birth to a dead chick didn't bother him. "It may not be to our taste," he said, "but buzzards just have to make do with what life dishes out." Three years ago I wrote a book describing twelve months my family and I spent in Australia. Soon after school closed in June this year, I planned to go back to Australia for a month. In return for a ticket I agreed to write articles for *Australian Way*, the in-flight magazine of Qantas airline. At the end of February, however, the editor of the magazine resigned to become a dancer. The next editor lasted six weeks before decamping to write the great Australian novel. Turbulence buffeted the magazine. By the time a third editor buckled herself into a seat and smoothed out a desk, arrangements with me had sunk out of sight. "We are changing the format of the magazine," she said on the telephone in May, "and don't know what kinds of articles we'll use. I hope you won't mind putting off your trip. When the new format is set, I'll get back in touch." "That's fine," I said, tired of being a begging nuisance, adding "best of luck" before putting the telephone down.

For a while I considered spending summer in Storrs. But early in June my bicycle was stolen. The theft upset me, and shortly afterward I reserved places for Vicki and myself on the ferry sailing from Portland, Maine, to Yarmouth, Nova Scotia. Vicki and her two brothers own a farm in Beaver River on the shore of the Bay of Fundy. I spent last summer in Nova Scotia, and the first essay in this collection describes that stay. After settling the children at camps in Maine, Vicki and I boarded the ferry. "What will you do in Nova Scotia?" Vicki asked, shutting the cabin door and handing me pajamas. "You wrote about everything last year." "Oh," I said, stretching out on the berth, "essayists portray passing, and I'll find things to describe."

I have now spent eight days in Beaver River. Mornings I work: chopping Japanese knotweed with a machete then prying up roots with a crowbar, sawing branches out of hawthorns and golden elders, climbing ladders and using a putty knife to free second-story windows sealed by paint, or carting off the chicken house that collapsed behind the barn a decade ago. While beams of the coop had sunk into the ground, a tent of Virginia creeper billowed over the lumber, its vines thick as wrists and taut as guy wires. I loaded remnants of the coop onto a big wheelbarrow, rolled them across the blueberry field, and pitched them over a stone wall into alders, throwing beams like a Scotsman tossing the caber. Getting rid of the chicken house took two days. Although each load of wood seemed a small lumberyard, I still made seventeen trips across the field. Deerflies had hatched, and they swirled about me like sawdust. Practically everything, however, is timber for the essayist's pen. Bird's-nest mushrooms grew on boards, the small cups tapered brown baskets, the mouths wide and the baskets overflowing with dusty spore cases resembling loaves of pita bread.

Despite spending a score of summers in Nova Scotia, I had not seen the mushroom before. Never does an observer clear-cut a landscape, even that inside a house. When Vicki was young, she slept in the Rose Room. Trellises of pink roses bloomed on the wallpaper while "Little Sarah," a chubby girl with stovepipe curls and wearing a blue dress, smiled contentedly from a Currier and Ives print, a marbled kitten cradled in her arms. Piled in a chest were Vicki's toys. Although I had rummaged through the chest in past summers, I had never really looked at the toys. On a white ceramic platter two and a half inches long and an inch and three-quarters wide lay a lobster, three green peas between its claws. For Sunday lunch Vicki's dolls could choose lobster or chicken, the latter brown and lying on a round dish, head lopped off and drumsticks thrust high in the air. For dessert Vicki served the dolls upside-down cake, covered with yellow and brown flecks looking like bits of apple and cinnamon. At the bottom of the chest sat a child's bank made out of iron. A pudgy man six inches tall slumped in a wicker porch chair, on the side of which was stamped TAMMANY BANK. A politician, the man sported a mustache and wore a black coat, yellow vest, and brown trousers. Black patent leather shoes stuck out from beneath the cuffs of the man's trousers, looking like slugs. Politics being rough, some of the paint on the man's forehead had been knocked loose, probably by angry constituents. The politician's right arm bent at a ninety-degree angle, the hand raised and fingers curled inward. A penny pushed into the hand rolled along the man's arm toward his chest and dropped through a slot into the chair.

In his autobiography *The Story of My Heart* (1883), Richard Jefferies, the British naturalist, wrote, "Time has never existed, and never will; it is purely an artificial arrangement. It is eternity now, it always was eternity, and always will be. . . . There is no separation—no past; eternity is NOW, is continuous." Spreading his arms, Jefferies lay "them on the sward," "seizing the grass," he explained, "to take the fullness of the days." Eternity is too abstract for my harrowing mind. Now, however, exists, and in my essays I plow, if not grass, at least the ripeness of hill and pasture, no matter the season. Every day I roam fields and woods in hopes of noticing Now.

In lamenting vanished pasts or dreaming of possible futures, people often miss Now. Before Slubey Garts buried folks in Carthage, he put apple seeds under their tongues. According to Welsh tale, the apple tree was the source not only of the fruit eaten by Adam and Eve but also of the wood used to make the cross on which Christ was crucified. God's mercy transformed the tree of the fall into the tree of the redemption. By putting pips in mouths, Slubey bound the past to the future and created an eternal or circular Now. My amblings in Nova Scotia go nowhere; yet they blossom, if not lightly with apples, at least with the heavy syrup of woodbine or European honeysuckle, the almond of one-flowered wintergreen, peppery lupin, and rugosa roses, the aroma sweeping across damp grass in a train.

The day I arrived at the farm I walked the lane leading to the bluff overlooking the bay. The headland was a palette dabbed with flowers: orange and yellow dripping from devil's paintbrush; cool blue vetch; and white whirling about ox-eyed daisies. In shrubs behind the headland, strips of purple lingered amid rhodora, and small constellations of flowers flickered weakly in Labrador tea. In peat beside the lane, field and wood horsetails resembled valances, slipshod with green whorls and falls. Spring azures sparked like switches, blue flashing on the downbeat of wings and vanishing on the upbeat. At the edge of "George's Field" yellow dash skippers perched on blades of grass. The butterflies resembled flakes of crust broken from the lips of pie pans. A red admiral stalked the side meadow, searching for females, his flight ragged, appearing doubting, not planned. Fritillaries settled on blackberry blossoms, their wings quivering like breaths. The wavering flights of butterflies brought my writing and human nature to mind. Winds of circumstance determine the saunterings of people and prose. Much as contradiction not only rends character but makes a person interesting, capable of vice one moment, virtue the next, so inconsistency forms the backbone of the essay.

Yesterday I walked early in the morning. Resembling a length of rug wool, a female garter snake lay in the grass along the lane, the head of a toad the size of a change purse clamped between her jaws. The toad's body bulged, looking rubbery as a deflated balloon. I sat in the grass a foot from the snake and watched her dine. "Why didn't you rescue the toad?" Vicki asked later. "I don't know," I said. Swallowing the toad took fifty-two minutes. Occasionally I stroked the sides of the snake. The first time I touched her she scythed slowly away. Later, however, the snake remained still when I touched her. To swallow the toad the snake dislocated her jaws. Afterward she curled then pushed the skin along her upper jaw outward before clamping down, the movement resembling a patient's raising his upper lip so a dentist could polish his teeth during a cleaning.

For most of the meal the toad moved its legs. Unfortunately the toad's hind legs dug into the ground and pushed him forward, thrusting him down the snake's gullet. Eventually the toad's front legs were pinned along its sides, looking like the arms of a cadet stiff at drill. Near the end of the meal the toad's back legs rose off the ground and stuck up, falling apart like the legs of an awkward middle-aged diver splashing into water, his belly sagging white and speckled. Finally as the snake pulled the body of the toad into its mouth, the legs straightened, the feet bowing out, resembling pliers slightly akimbo. Once the toad became a bulge behind the snake's head, she flicked her tongue, seeming to notice me for the first time. When I chucked her under the chin, she turned and poured herself through ferns and out of sight. I stood and walked to the headland. For the next sixteen minutes I watched bumblebees gathering nectar from hedge bindweed. After the walk I turned on the radio and heard a preacher in Halifax say, "It's as easy to go to Hell from a university as it is from a booze joint or a gambling net."

Unlike Jefferies who wandered wood and field partly to escape what he called "every day existence," I tether my ordinary doings to those of nature. Often I fail. Sometimes my descriptions of flowers and trees blossom stiffly like wallpaper. Other times observations run out of my mind like rain. One morning after studying butterflies, I rushed home to describe what I saw to Vicki. Vicki had just finished bathing. "Ah," she said, standing, soap bubbles sliding off her, "Venus Rising from the Tub." Butterflies suddenly molted out of mind. Later that day a letter arrived from Eliza. "Crew started this morning and was a lot of fun even though my arms were really sore after," she wrote. "Guess what? I got up on water skis yesterday! I signed up for a beginner's class. It took me three times, but I finally did it. Unfortunately I didn't stay up too long, but I'm going to keep on trying until I can go all the way around the lake without falling. Tomorrow I'm going to pottery then try out for a part in the camp play *Cinderella*. I'm still swimming a quarter mile every day. I am so busy!"

Tomorrow I plan to saw dead wood out of the sycamore maples by the front fence. I don't know what I will do afterward, but certainly matters worthy of a sentence or two will pass by and I'll be busy. I hope readers' days will be just as full. The ragged colt, Slubey Garts said, often proves a good horse. If these essays entertain and bring smiles and perhaps appreciation for Now and the circles we all trot, then I will have proved a pretty good nag.

Deprived of Unhappiness

Five Summers

"*I*t's the day you were married,"
Vicki said when I asked the date. In the paper that evening I read
about a man in New Mexico who blamed his philandering on a UFO.
"I was sitting at a bar drinking Coors," he said, "when suddenly a
white light blinded me. The next morning I awoke in a motel beside
a strange woman. Like me all the woman remembered from the night
before was the light. Aliens abducted us, and when they finished
studying us, they dropped us in the motel." Two days later Francis's
new mountain bike was stolen. Francis chained the bicycle to the rack
outside the university bookstore. A car with two men drove past. On
seeing the bicycle, the driver stopped. One of the men hopped out,
looked at the bicycle, then told the driver to park. From the trunk of
the car the driver removed bolt cutters. While the first man held the
bicycle, the driver cut the lock, after which they stuffed the bicycle
in the car and drove away. People shouted at them, but the men paid
no attention. "Doped to the gills," a woman said. Two observers jotted down the number of the car's license plate. Within twenty minutes campus police traced the car to an owner in Danielson. The man
had given the car to his daughter for the day. She in turn lent it to her
boyfriend, a junkie with warrants out for his arrest "all over Eastern
Connecticut," a policeman said. The thieves drove to Willimantic
and sold the bicycle in Windham Heights for drug money. Shortly afterward both men went to ground, one eventually turning up in a rehabilitation clinic in Norwich, the other surfacing in Arizona. The
theft upset Vicki. "The man who owns an empty chicken coop," my

friend Josh said, "doesn't have to worry about the fox." Josh's remark did not satisfy Vicki. "What has happened to Storrs?" she said. "I don't think I want to live here anymore." The time had come for us to go to Nova Scotia.

Vicki and I had not been to the farm in Beaver River for five summers. Each June we discussed going but always decided against the trip. Vicki's mother is difficult. "Oh, God!" Vicki once exclaimed, "suppose I find Mother waiting for me at the Pearly Gates. She would make heaven hell." Although Vicki's mother said she intended to go to Nova Scotia each summer, she never made the trip. As a result we stayed away, and the house stood empty. This summer at the end of June Vicki and I dropped the children at camp in Maine and took the ferry to Yarmouth.

We landed on a sunny morning. Lupin rumpled purple and pink across small hills. Near Hebron a marsh hawk flew over the road, a snake twisting in its claws. "Five summers with the length of five long winters," I said, paraphrasing the English poet William Wordsworth, "and I again see the landscape rolling with a soft, inland murmur." Before unpacking the car, Vicki and I walked around the house, George and Penny, the dogs, following us, tails switching. In the side yard blossoms dangled like earrings from the golden chaintree, and a bouquet of bridal wreath leaned against the bay window. Blue flag bloomed in the damp, and leggy buttercups stood waist-high. By the well cover moneywort curled through grass, its blossoms polished and orange. Under the willow a bale of bedstraw sprawled loose and tangled. Tall dock draped over the bedstraw, flowers spilling from the stalks like rain. By August flowers on the dock were crimson, each blossom resembling a spiny red shield, edged with green. From the middle of the shields oozed scarlet drops shaped like tongues.

Between the ribs of the chicken house clumps of dame's rocket bulged, minute purple ditches draining through the white petals into green wells at the centers of the flowers. Behind dame's rocket stretched a hedge of roses, perfume billowing from them in a fog. Familiar, the flowers made me feel part of place, a green, vital community, one, however, inhabited by few people. During our eight weeks in Nova Scotia, the telephone rang just fourteen times. Three of the calls came from Jack Porter the plumber while another was an advertisement promoting economical long-distance calling. With the exception of a report from camp describing Eliza's asthma, the rest of the calls were from Vicki's brothers discussing repairs to the house. Instead of life's being a patchwork of matters accomplished, days in Nova Scotia seemed a fabric of things not done. At first Vicki missed the jangle of Connecticut. After eight days in Nova Scotia, she looked at the dogs and said, "I couldn't make it here without them." "I know I'm not exciting," I said examining a sprig of heal-all on the kitchen table, the spire resembling a minute hive, the bud cells sealed with blue wax, "but a woman doesn't marry a man because he is thrilling." "Shit!" Vicki exclaimed, "that was my mistake."

Holes speckled the barn. Throws of porcupine pellets slid across the woodshed, while mouse droppings lay scattered through the house like chaff on a threshing floor. Flashing had curled away from the chimney, and molding had cracked and slipped from parlor ceilings. Twenty years ago, when paintings of ships sailed across walls and floors shone like leather, the house seemed a museum. For Vicki memories of better, neater times undermined present happiness. Never having seen the house in its best days, I settled comfortably into routine. A bundle of walking sticks leaned against a wall in the shed. I found my stick immediately, my hand wrapping smoothly around it as if five summers had not passed. Almost without thought I lit the kitchen stove, then walked down the lane to the bluff and gathered a bushel of driftwood for kindling.

Despite the years not much had changed. Groves of alders pocked the blueberry field, and white spruce and tamarack had rooted and grown weedy. Porcupines killed the horse chestnut by the shed. Before eating breakfast, Vicki and I used to watch warblers glean the tree, flickering through the branches like light bulbs. When porcupines began girdling maples in the front yard, our neighbor Bill Grace shot seven. They had dens, he said, under the chicken house. Aside from automobiles and great horned owls, few creatures prey upon porcupines in southwest Nova Scotia. At dusk in the damp spruce woods, I occasionally stumbled upon porcupines. On seeing me, porcupines hauled themselves into trees, swaying like shaggy black sacks attached to ropes. At first the dogs did not notice porcupines, and not until August did I long for a family of fishers to settle the property.

Late one August afternoon Vicki and I and the dogs walked along the bluff at Bear Cove. Abruptly George tumbled over a ledge. He barked twice and thrashed through brush. Then aside from the scolding of a pair of juncos, the day became quiet. "Jesus!" Vicki exclaimed, "he has fallen off the bluff." We stood quietly for a moment. Then I heard George scrambling upward. When he pulled into sight, he shook his head back and forth. In his mouth was what appeared to be a rodent bristling with white and black fur. Instead George chewed porcupine. Barbed, the quills work into flesh, and if not extracted, kill. "Because of porcupines, I have shot four of my dogs," Emile, an acquaintance, said. "Vets cost more than dogs." While Vicki pulled out quills, I sat on George, clamping my hands around his muzzle like a vice. The quills did not slip free easily. Blood spurted, and George writhed. Vicki removed thirty-four quills. Thirty thousand quills blanket a full-grown porcupine. "Only .12% of a porcupine's quills," I said to Vicki that night; "we should be thankful George isn't much trencherman." "Unlike students, dogs are educable," my friend Josh interrupted when I told him about George and the porcupine in September. "Once a human begins sticking his nose into the ass-end of anything, he never stops, no matter the number of quills." Josh overrated George and spoke before I finished my account. The next afternoon as Vicki and I sat on the porch, George suddenly ran out of the woods, his nose studded with fourteen quills. For suburban dogs porcupine is addictive. The following day while Vicki and I walked along the headland, Penny darted down a path and vanished into the spruce woods. When she reappeared, her mouth resembled a sardine can, the top rolled back and up, bristling with quills not fish bones, and dripping blood rather than oil. After I grabbed Penny and forced her mouth wider, Vicki ripped the quills out. Blood made the quills slippery, and several snapped. I jammed the heel of my right palm across Penny's mouth and carried her back to the house. Once there I held her flat on the kitchen table while Vicki shined a flashlight down her throat and teased the broken quills out with tweezers.

The dogs were not the only inquisitive creatures who bled during the summer. Five years ago I hacked paths through brush to favorite spots on the farm: the middle of the quaking bog, the spruce woods, and the rhubarb wall. I imagined readers of my essays following my footsteps and discovering traces of paragraphs. Paths last no longer than books. One path had vanished, and blackberry canes roiled across the other two like razor wire. On the second day, however, canes did not stop me from bludgeoning along paths searching for the familiar. Unfortunately I wore shorts. That night I measured forty-nine and three-quarters inches of hard red slices on my left leg and thirty-eight inches on my right, plus yards of welts and a sewing box brimming with button-shaped scabs. Later in the summer I cleared two of the paths and cut a new path from the side meadow through alder and elderberry to Ma's Property west of the house. Early in July, though, the paths seemed emblems both of the evanescence and the fecundity of life.

A tangle of brambly days swiftly obscures marks people leave behind, blossoms and sharp thorns filling indentations of toe and heel. Almost as if seeking reassurance, I wandered the property. Recognizing plants created the illusion of permanence. Like life itself my rambles were not planned, and without thinking I fell into roaming, much as I had drifted into family and teaching. During July and August I walked every day, usually for three hours but occasionally for five. Repetition made the walks important in some way that lay beyond explanation. Quoting Wordsworth, I told Vicki that by summer's end I would "see into the life of things." That did not happen. Instead of probing deeply, I stayed on the surface and observed the days.

Penny and George accompanied me, and often I sat and watched them. In the woods red squirrels buried cones under the roots of spruce. The dogs tried to flush out squirrels, Penny snapping roots with her teeth and George pulling his hind legs under him while he dug, his body resembling the curved end of a paper clip. Although squirrels often broke from the ground, the dogs were not quick enough to catch them. In August the dogs ate pails of blueberries, and some days I had to push them out of patches with my walking stick. For the dogs, walks offered opportunities to roll in fragrant delights. George particularly enjoyed lathering in the remains of crabs picked apart by gulls. One afternoon at Beaver River he showered in the body of a harbor seal. The seal had been decapitated, the head having been torn rather than sliced off so that the animal's neck resembled a turtleneck sweater turned inside out. For her part, Penny preferred bird droppings to dead animals. After walks I scrubbed the dogs with bay leaves.

Because I recognized them, flowers did not seem wild but almost arranged, shaped like memory turned into story. Instead, however, of marking sentence and paragraph, wildflowers punctuated vision, creating the impression of a comfortable, orderly world. In early July, flowers bloomed along the lane like crisp simple sentences: chokeberry; tall red clover; king devil, the white froth of spittlebugs milky on stems, sometimes five or six insects to a stem; yellow cinquefoil; sandwort; star flower; and vetch climbing through grass in ladders, then bursting into blue lanterns. While stamens in blossoms of Labrador tea resembled cant hooks, those in sheep laurel seemed ribs pushing the blossoms into bowls.

A bunchberry blossom looked like a serving tray, twenty-seven green goblets perched on it, from the top of each goblet a red swizzle stick leaning out of sudsy black froth. Twin flowers nodded above moss at the edge of woods, the insides of the blossoms teased, wispy as cotton candy. In damp spots pitcher plants bloomed, the flowers ornate as Victorian lampshades. Along the bluff blossomed sundrops; creeping blackberry; plantain; constellations of blue-eyed grass; cranberry; lady's mantle, its minute green flowers, loose tatting; and yellow rattle, the corolla a snout opening to the side and tinged with purple dark as a blood blister. In daylight ox-eyed daisies seeped out of sight. At night, however, the blooms on the daisies rose pale and luminous up stems.

Early in July I roamed dusk and evening. Late in afternoons fog blew across the blueberry field, billowing through alders like blankets flapping on a clothesline. Off Port Maitland the sea resembled pewter, and the foghorn exhaled, sounding bronchial and congested. I liked the cool evenings, but not foggy mornings when the sun lurked just behind the hour like a hot anvil. After dinner fireflies flashed along the lane, in the mist flickering like wicks before dying and turning black. On misty nights in Storrs fireflies exploded like Roman candles, popping in luminous staccato bursts. Vicki said the sky was higher in Nova Scotia than in Connecticut, where hills reached upward and trees hovered over houses like nursemaids. Many evenings I stood on the headland and watched the sun set. On foggy days the sun closed like an inflamed eye, the light strained and runny. Sometimes clouds turned purple and bruised the sky, red seeping through then welling bloody from bone. Often night closed day like an aged Venetian blind, the slats bent and dangling loosely from ladder tapes, allowing slivers of light to slide though the dark, yellow and pink, orange and silver.

One night in August the ocean seemed smooth as a dining room table. Over the table fog hung soft as silk. Instead of staining the distance, golden sunlight unrolled and slid in a carpet across the water to the shore. Early in July, vapor trails glowed then spread into fibrous seams. On clear nights lights in Port Maitland glared fat and yellow, and beams from the lighthouse at Cape St. Mary diced the dark. On such nights streams oozing from the guzzle at Bartlett's Beach gleamed like oil. Some evenings the sand itself seemed chrome, the stones above the beach tarnished in comparison. In July, lights from boats fishing for herring pricked the horizon. One night I counted twenty-three boats. Above them hung a crimson slice of moon. When breezes were strong, plants on the headland bent over trimmed and brushed. Gulls skidded sideways, dipped, and muscled up the beach toward Port Maitland. When nights were stormy, breaking waves resembled pages torn from spiral notebooks, the middle of each page pulling free and rolling toward the top and bottom of the leaf simultaneously. On calm evenings waves sizzled forward then, tumbling back, hooked stones that popped like fat.

Inland, night winds pushed shrubs and caught on trees, rasping and sliding around the house like straw brooms. On the headland I struggled against the temptation to think. In open spaces thoughts become abstract. Words drift toward stars and losing contact with sustaining dirt foster illusion. In woods open spaces are small. When thoughts begin to soar skyward, a broken branch snags them and punctures illusion. I think best in woods where limbs restrict the movement of mind. Confined, a person notices the immediate. Ideas do not swell to fill emptiness but instead root and sometimes flower.

In July I spent much time in the boggy woods behind Ma's Property. Over a decade ago boys built a hut in the woods, stripping signs from Route One in order to construct the roof and walls. Wondering if the hut had vanished like my paths, I explored the woods the day after we arrived. In a clearing, spruce toppled against each other, opening a funnel to the sky. At the edge of the clearing a great horned owl sat atop a shattered tree. The owl stared at me for a moment then turned and rolled away through the spruce. Beneath the tree lay a pellet as large as a chicken egg.

Time shrank the hut. Mushrooms grew in beds on the roof, and lichens splattered the walls. Youth, however, remained vital, as another group of children had moved in, painting "Boys In The Hood" and "Stay Out Or Die" over doors, after this last phrase adding their initials, S.D., J.D., J.R., C.M., T.M., B.G., and Eli B. Scattered across the floor of the hut were a brown eyeglass case, several playing cards, and nubs of yellow candles, these last, I assumed, the paraphernalia of mystic doings.

I examined the cards. On the four of hearts a circus dog balanced atop a ball. The dog wore a red and yellow hat shaped like a sailboat and a yellow and green striped shirt with a red ruffle around the neck. In his left paw the dog grasped a red balloon. Circus performers appeared on all the cards. On the eleven of stars a woman wearing pink tights and a soapy smile sat on a trapeze, in her lap a ball with the number eleven painted on it. Under rusty bedsprings I found a water-logged textbook. Entitled *New Worlds* and published by Ginn in Toronto, the book, a label declared, was "THE PROPERTY OF THE DEPARTMENT OF EDUCATION, PROVINCE OF NOVA SCOTIA." Although a rocket resembling a mechanical pencil blasted across the cover toward the sky, the book was an elementary reader containing a miscellany of short pieces. "A Fleck of Mould" described Alexander Flemming's discovery of penicillin while "Quills" told the improbable story of a porcupine's escaping a hungry fisher. Floating above the first paragraph of "The Kingdom of the Tides" was an aquarium of sea creatures, clam worms, squid, and crabs, among others. Cousins of shrimp, barnacles, students learned, were eaten by aborigines in Australia. "Wings Across the Atlantic" described the flight of a Vimy Vickers from Newfoundland to Ireland in 1919. The plane cost fifty thousand dollars, and the flight lasted sixteen hours and twelve minutes, each minute, I calculated, costing $51.44.

I sauntered through the woods almost every day. Snowberry crept demurely across moss, and on damp mornings the leaves of Clintonia splayed glistening across the ground. In August lady's slippers shriveled into seed, the flowers drying into brown scythes. In July butter-cups splashed across glades, and wood sorrel glowed pink and yellow. At the edge of Ma's Property field speedwell curled through the shadow of a stone wall, the white petals striped with blue. Through-out the woods wild sarsaparilla rolled upward into green wheels. One plant burrowed under bark on a rotting tree, fourteen and a half inches off the ground, and rooting pushed out runners that wound behind the bark for another five inches before spinning into the light. By early August yellow splotched the leaves of sarsaparilla. Later the yellow rusted, and black dots of fungus peppered the leaves.

Often I munched the birchy roots of sarsaparilla. On walks I chewed the leaves of many plants: bay, Labrador tea, wild mint, and at the end of the summer, goldenrod. I also ate bushels of berries, along the bluff in July wild strawberries, then for a month blueberries, and finally blackberries at the end of August. Worms and stinkbugs sea-soned the berries. The worms were soft and tasteless, and I swallowed them. Nothing, however, spoils berries quicker than a dollop of stink-bugs. I also sampled black crowberries and cranberries, the former bland and the latter bitter. Bunchberries were more water than flavor. Clintonia berries tasted green. Supposedly the berries were poisonous, and after crushing a cupful against my palate, I rinsed my mouth with sarsaparilla berries. I also sampled the stems of plants. When I felt dozy, I chewed Indian pipes. Because I experienced no bad effects from Clintonia, I tried the stems of Indian tobacco. That was a mistake. In-dian tobacco really is poisonous. The stems seared my mouth, and for a while I worried that my throat would swell and I would suffocate.

The person who roams wood and field eventually becomes willful, clambering over fences, both those taut with wire and those fash-ioned out of barbed common sense. For years I have bolted from pad-docks of platitude and good advice. Instead of confining, the words *do not* invite me to trespass. In hopes of tasting and thinking anew, I disobey warnings. Still, no matter where I wander, my meals remain the conventional produce of stove and icebox. On the path curving along the headland lay pheasant droppings round as my thumb. The droppings were a batter of seeds and undigested blueberries and sar-saparilla berries. The blend fermented, and the droppings smelled like apples. Soaked in heavy cream, they would have made a rich dessert, and I longed to sample them. Alas, I did not taste them. "And a good thing, too," Vicki said. "What would the children think if they learned you ate birdshit?" My favorite berries came from shadbush or Indian pear. Almond-flavored seeds added grit to the berries. In August I boiled a tub of blueberries and shadbush berries into jelly. Every night I slathered it over biscuits. Vicki tasted the jelly and after praising it as "splendid" never ate it again.

Parts of the woods resembled florists' shops. Cinnamon ferns arched into vases, sterile leaves forming enameled sides. Within each vase stood shafts of fertile leaves, bundles of spore cases hanging from leaflets, each case a minute ball. When the cases split and spores tumbled out, light shone through the cases, turning them bronze. Later in the summer the shafts of fertile leaves snapped, and the leaflets sagged like sails rotting in the doldrums. On interrupted ferns shafts of fertile leaves bent over, almost as if the roots had been cut. Too weak to be satisfied with noticing, the human mind dissects observation then constructs thoughts. Thoughts function like crutches. When people lose belief in certitude, thought supports and steadies them, preventing them from tumbling into a meaningless world chaotic with sensation.

At first when I looked at ferns, I saw emblems, not the ferns themselves. Shafts of cinnamon ferns reminded me of broken columns raised above the graves of men who died prematurely while the shafts of interrupted ferns recalled roses wilting above the graves of young women. Outside the woods cinnamon ferns did not grow into emblems. Behind Black Point winds blew through the peat bog, drying ferns so that they seemed metallic and rough as graters. By August, ferns on Black Point crinkled inward, looking burned. In contrast ferns in woods remained damp and green. Many ferns grew in the woods: spinulose wood fern, pools of New York fern yellow in the sunlight, and near stone walls lady fern, the plants resembling showy bonnets, filigrees of fruit dots decorating the leaves. Stalks of bracken resembled quirts. Sometimes I lay beneath bracken and imagined the leaves above me a green sky.

During the first week in Beaver River I had a few chores. At the end of his last summer in Nova Scotia, Vicki's father forgot to remove the mailbox from the roadside, and a snow plow crumpled it. One morning I drove to Home Hardware and bought a new box, a "RURAL MAILBOX" costing $14.49 and manufactured by Steel City Corporation in Youngstown, Ohio. I spent another morning cutting high grass around the barn, being careful not to swing the scythe into my leg. Vicki's father's favorite tree was the tamarack, and that afternoon I removed three saplings from the blueberry field and planted them at the edge of the windbreak beyond the side meadow. I named the trees after Vicki's father: Edward, Dudley, and Hume. At the end of the summer Edward and Hume were thriving, but Dudley had lost needles, this despite being moved with a ball of dirt around its roots much bigger than those about the roots of the other two trees and my planting it in what seemed the best location, sunny, yet damp enough so that it would not require watering.

For five years mice treated the house as both graveyard and playing field. After sweeping up a peck of droppings, Vicki and I disinterred corpses from drawers and tossed them into the roses. At the bottom of a bottle, once part of a medicine chest on a clipper ship, a mouse collapsed into a ridge of fur, marbled by decay and sprinkled with white dots. Another mouse hung over the back of a drawer, slack as an empty bag. Fingers of fur poked into boxes, and small skeletons curled inside balls of yarn. One mouse died at midfield on "Spear's Jolly Game of Blow Football." The field was six and a half inches wide and eleven and a quarter inches long. Wire goalposts stood at each end of the field. Behind the goalposts holes gaped. In front of each goal stood a metallic player three inches tall. The player at the left end of the field wore shorts, a long-sleeved red shirt, and black socks with two red stripes at the top, while the player at the right end wore a blue shirt. Plastic straws accompanied the game, the object being to blow a ping-pong ball past the opponent's player through the goal into the hole. The drawer contained cheering sections of fans, the larvae of dermestid beetles. Vicki thought the larvae repulsive. Never had I found the larvae in a house, and I thought about taking some back to Connecticut. Keeping them fed would have been easy. Every evening Bill Grace's cat hunted the lane, and hardly a day passed during which I did not find the body of a meadow vole or a short-tailed shrew.

Insects have intrigued me since childhood. A hornet's landing on my arm stirs curiosity, not fear. By the middle of July black flies had almost disappeared. Still, after dinner one night I counted eighteen red welts on Penny's belly. I took a fly net to Nova Scotia and wore it on walks. On one walk the net slumped against the right side of my head, and so many flies bit me that my ear puffed, looking like, Vicki said, a red eggplant. Throughout the summer my neck resembled a gravel pit, hard with proud welts. Instead of shirts with sailboats tacking across chests, the Department of Tourism, Vicki said, should distribute shirts with ovals stamped on the fronts. Surrounding the oval would be the words "Welcome to Nova Scotia." In the middle of the oval would appear a platter, a human resembling a cooked lobster stretched across it. Hovering above the human and wearing a bib and holding a hollow needle shaped like a syringe should be a huge black fly. "Spray yourself with Raid," George Hall suggested. "That's what I do in the summer, and the flies leave me alone." Raid also kept mosquitoes off, George said. Mosquitoes sailed after me on all my walks, bumping against me whenever I stood still. Occasionally I let a mosquito feed. Most appeared to be salt marsh mosquitoes.

Environment influences behavior. For the entire summer the toilet remained an object of aesthetic contemplation. "You mean that you did not use the john once," Josh said. "Porcupines, tent caterpillars, and humans relieve themselves in their nests, something I find repulsive," I said. "This summer I decided to elevate my life, taking advantage of the moss behind the windbreak." "Good for you," Josh exclaimed; "I know people in New York who pay six or seven hundred dollars a day to return to nature and poop in the woods." Living elegantly was occasionally inconvenient, especially during Hurricane Bertha. In the second week in July deerflies appeared. Happily, deerflies preferred dog to human. During one walk I swatted fourteen flies from George's back and pinched eight from Penny's head, popping them between my thumb and index finger, the blood spurting and staining Penny's head like measles.

The hedge of roses bordering the side meadow bloomed with insects: among others, bumblebees, lacewings, and small flies resembling slivers of gold. At times the willow became a bird feeder. After the caterpillars grew plump, warblers harvested mourning cloak larvae. Some mornings a robin flew into the willow and using her bill like a fork tossed caterpillars onto the ground where she dined, as Vicki put it, "on a green tablecloth." Herds of aphids grazed leaves at the tips of twigs, molting and leaving crumpled white skins behind. The larvae of ladybugs ate the aphids, and one afternoon I counted twenty-two larvae in six minutes. In the middle of the day the larvae dozed; mornings, however, they were hungry, chewing aphids eagerly, the meals wiggling, other aphids on the twigs oblivious to the banquet. I spent hours watching the larvae. Stitched along the left and right side of each larva was a row of five orange mounds. In the middle of the larva's back were four smaller lumps. Like aphids the ladybugs molted, and their shells dried and curled, looking as if they were rolling down the leaves. Although the larvae did not move quickly, watching them entertained me. Because I was still, I saw other creatures: a pickerel frog under the well cover, then, on the stump of the horse chestnut, yellow snails the size of earrings. Under the grill lurked a toad plump as a purse, the gold around its eyes coins. Early in August small crickets swarmed through the meadow. Almost simultaneously schools of toadlets appeared, and one morning I counted forty-six in twelve minutes.

When a person is still, life stirs. One afternoon as I sat on the porch, a pine sawyer tumbled into my lap. I scooped him up in my right hand and extended my index finger. He crawled to the end of my finger, perched for a moment above my nail, flexing his wings, then lumbered into the air toward the windbreak. Immediately afterward, a female pelecinid landed on the wall behind me. Divided into six segments, the abdomen of the pelecinid appeared lengths of pipe joined by flexible connections. Jabbing its abdomen into the ground, the pelecinid lays eggs in grubs. Until I slipped a finger beneath its body and the insect clung to my hand, the pelecinid rested on the wall, its upper legs pulled back from the wood, but its abdomen and thick hind legs forming a black tripod.

Exploring the familiar side yard invigorated days. Meadowsweet bloomed at the end of July. Handfuls of tiny beetles banqueted on the spires. From a distance the beetles, their backs dusty and flecked with yellow pollen, looked like seeds. In the middle of August red dragonflies hovered over the blossoms. The slender abdomens of the insects sliced the air, opening narrow cuts. On a maple a tussock moth caterpillar lay in a fissure of bark. An orange skullcap clung to the cater-pillar's head; behind it four clumps of white bristles swept upward like brooms in a rack. At the edge of the blueberry field beetles bored into spruce. Resin dripped from their holes and washed down bark like skim milk. Often the resin curdled, at first appearing white but even-tually going off and turning yellow. Amid streams of resin insects spun clots of cocoons. In the windbreak bud caps perched jauntily atop twigs. In May, larvae of spruce moths hatched and bored under the bud caps where they fed on the soft needles. Using silk, the larvae constructed shelters by stitching the caps to the needles. Eventually larvae grew out of their houses and moved down the twigs to graze on fresh needles. Slightly smaller than the tip of my little finger, the caps glowed like small red bulbs, but like many things that lurked close to hand and eye, I hadn't noticed them before.

Every summer I noticed spiders. Gray cross spiders wove webs in windows. Webs stretched from the ridge of the roof to the chimney, the sunlight hammering them into thin, wrought-iron struts. At night I stood on the bed upstairs and watched the pedal and key work of spinning. On windy evenings webs snapped in quiet timpani. One night a yellow bear tumbled into a web. Before the moth could es-cape, a spider seized his head. The moth beat his wings furiously. At first the wings resembled feathers fluttering in a draft. Later they seemed blades of a fan, the governor of which had broken.

Many mornings I wandered the property before webs dried and became invisible. Along the lane and in George's Field webs of grass spiders lay against each other like pieces of a crazy quilt that had come unbound. At times I thought the webs paragraphs, those of orb weavers neoclassical, polished and elegant, the others gothic and chaotic. Webs of comb-footed spiders looked like loose boxes, the lines of the webs never curving but forming snarls of triangles and rhombuses. Like the unruly prose of popular writers, the webs were just as effective, I thought, as those of orb weavers. "The trouble with your writing," Josh once said, "is that you try to lure readers to thought. Stop spinning radii. Light a candle hot with sex and violence, and you'll catch moths enough to pad a bankroll." In the boggy woods reddish-brown orb weavers clung to their webs until midmorning. The spiders were so small that when they scurried over my hands I could not feel them. White and brown, the abdomen of the other orb weaver common in the woods resembled a nub of vanilla ice cream, on the top of which a drop of fudge had fallen and hardened.

In mid-August when winged ants congregated in ant mounds, shamrock spiders became noticeable. Attached to bay and meadowsweet, their webs hung one or two feet off the ground. In the morning the webs gleamed like mother of pearl. Instead of remaining in webs, spiders lurked under leaves pulled into rough cabanas. If I held my hand under a cabana then thumped the retreat lightly, spiders dropped into my palm. One morning I examined a quart of spiders, enough, I reckoned, for a meal. Twice as big as shadbush berries, the abdomens looked tasty, and I asked Vicki if she would cook spiders for me. "Season them the way you think best," I said, adding that I thought they would fry nicely in olive oil. Alas, the spiders got no closer to the kitchen table than the bird droppings, and I had to content myself with study. Actually that was good enough. With long candy-cane legs and orange or sometimes yellow abdomens speckled with white, the spiders were lovely as sunsets.

The white dots on the spiders' backs resembled stars, a constellation of gulls, one flying behind another. Looking at the dots, I remembered the tale of Larus, the slave of Hephastus. Elegant and fastidious while Hephastus was comfortable in soot, Larus thought himself superior to his master. When Venus asked his help in arranging her tryst with Mars, Larus obliged. On discovering the part his slave played in Venus's adultery, Hephastus decided to kill Larus. So that Larus could escape Hephastus's anger, Venus changed Larus into a seagull. Because he was lame, Hephastus could not catch Larus when the slave jumped into the air. The blacksmith of the gods, Hephastus was strong, however, and before Larus flew out of sight, Hephastus threw a shovelful of live coals after him. One of the coals landed on Larus's back and singed his feathers, thus creating the black-backed gull.

At times I thought the inside of our house a web, one woven by mice, however, not spiders. Mice shredded bars of soap and chewed ends off a serving fork and spoon, drilling for oil that had seeped into the wood from forty summers of salads. Upstairs mice gnawed a hole through the bottom of a chart chest that had floated unscathed through years on the sea. Inside the chest mice chewed charts into nests. When I opened the chest, the aroma of urine seemed etched in the wood. I took the charts outside and dried them on the well cover. Mice had munched paths over the world. Close to home, they nibbled through the Bay of Fundy, following a chart based upon a survey undertaken by Captain P. F. Shortland in 1862. After chewing across the Grand Manan Channel, making a landfall at the southwest head of Grand Manan Island, they thrashed through Mickle Shoal and up the coast to Bradford Cove where they wandered inland to Benson Creek.

Only a few mice were domestic, most preferring to sail far from Nova Scotia. Many traveled the East India Archipelago. Following a chart describing "Eastern Passages to China and Japan," published by James Imray in 1884, one wanderer nibbled into the Strait of Macassar, then turned west toward Borneo and churned through Sumpug Bay, only to vanish at the foot of Mt. Mandalia. For furry adventurers mountains were mousetraps. After going ashore at Pt. Dialao on Luzon Island in the Philippines, another traveler disappeared on the slopes of Mt. Pascan, 7624 feet high, according to a chart describing the "Western Route to China," published in 1879. Following the second chart marking the same route, another mouse grounded on Alligator Island in the Singapore Strait. Still, the mishap did not tear the bottom out of the voyage. The mouse, however, was a poor navigator, and shortly after refloating, wrecked his adventure on High Point on Battam Island.

Man is self-serving, forever confusing virtue with inclination. Because genes have made me inconsistent, I condemn consistency, seeing it a comfortable retreat sought by folks unable to stomach the rich broth of life. And so despite having found the side meadow diverse enough to sustain a lifetime of voyages, I sat upon the well cover and dreamed of wandering far from rose and willow, family and Beaver River. During the spring tides I sailed south of Bangkok through the Gulf of Siam, sounding depths with a dipsey lead. From seventeen to thirty-six fathoms the bottom was often a mixture of mud and shells or soft mud. On another voyage I sailed the coast of China between "Formosa Island and Pe-Chi-Li Gulf." South of Van Dieman Strait, I studied the outlines of islands: Suwa, a volcano rising above white cliffs then exploding in a cloud of smoke, and the Kusakaki Rocks, teeth worn into cavities by centuries of overbite.

Twenty-four miles out of Port Natal, I first saw the light flashing at Cape Natal. Near the mouth of the Buffalo River in British Kafraria, I visited the "Proposed Township" of East London, seeing the Flagstaff, Wharf, and Cattle Kraal. Of course I'm not a real adventurer. Because of a note pasted on a chart describing the "Western Route to China" (1883), I avoided the Sunda Strait. "Caution," the note warned. "In consequence of Volcanic Eruptions having taken place in Sunda Strait the charts of the locality are probably incorrect in many particulars. The Great Channel may be unchanged, but the channels between Krakatoa and Seboeko are blocked and there is much floating pumice." Even though Vicki and the children and I recently spent a year in Australia, I did not sail the "unsurveyed coast" northwest of Cape York Peninsula. Despite having snorkeled along the Great Barrier Reef three summers ago, I avoided the area around the Reef because a chart declared it "unexamined and considered dangerous navigation."

Four hours of tossing on the well cover were enough. Despite occasionally being swept out of domesticity by the riptide of dream, I am an onshore mariner, most comfortable sailing the placid waters of routine. In Nova Scotia rarely does the unexpected disrupt a day. As soon as Vicki and I arrived in Nova Scotia, we slipped into a well-trod furrow. In July we ate strawberries every day. One day a week we ate fish, another day, rappie pie. On Fridays we shopped in Yarmouth, stopping at Minard's Bakery on the way to town and buying sugar doughnuts. The doughnuts were warm when we bought them, and we each ate two. From Minard's we drove to the Bank of Montreal and withdrew money for shopping. Afterward we went to the liquor store and bought four bottles of wine. In Connecticut Vicki and I don't drink much wine. In Nova Scotia we always had one or two glasses at dinner. During the summer we drank twenty-six bottles of wine, ten white and sixteen red. Aside from the trip to Yarmouth each week and visits to the Shore Grocery in Port Maitland two miles away, Vicki and I rarely left Beaver River.

To add imaginative zest to the summer and create the delusion that we were sophisticated travelers, we bought wines from around the world. On warm nights we sat on the well cover and wandered vineyards in California, France, Canada, Chile, Italy, Argentina, Portugal, Australia, and South Africa. Around the vineyards, however, I raised a fence. Never did we scale elevated heights of price. Instead we kept to the lowlands, never paying more than ten dollars Canadian or seven dollars American for a bottle of wine. Unlike me Vicki found the fence confining, and occasionally she sat on the top rail. One Friday, for example, the bottles she selected cost $9.93, $9.95, $9.97, and $9.98.

After buying wine, I drove to the Yarmouth Mall. While Vicki bought groceries at Sobey's, I roamed stores eavesdropping on conversations. Once I heard a crank say that fish roe flushed dark spots from the brain. Recently I had felt, if not dark, at least gloomy, so I bought a twenty-four-ounce bottle of cod liver oil. Every morning thereafter I swallowed a tablespoonful of oil before breakfast. The fishy fragrance repulsed Vicki, and she said I was poisoning myself; the livers of fish, she explained, not only filtered blood but also became repositories of poison.

When I tired of eavesdropping, I bought a Halifax newspaper and read it while eating a chocolate ice cream cone. I read the paper every day, on days other than Fridays purchasing a copy at the Shore Grocery. Reading did not take long. Order strikes me as a fiction, and I no longer read from front to back. Nowadays I read from back to front, though sometimes I vary routine by starting my reading in the middle of a newspaper. Educators argue that reading influences life, a claim I think suspect. Still, not wanting the way I read newspapers to turn life beyond the page disorderly, I forced system upon my reading and studied obituaries, writing the names of graveyards in a notebook.

A line of hills rolled across the nomenclature of cemeteries: Pleasant, Camp, Laurel, Rose, Fern, Pine, Forest, Sandy, and Hardwood Hill. Slightly more elevated than hills themselves were Hilltop and Hillcrest. Mount Olivet and Mount Pleasant were even higher; their slopes, however, were soft, and repentant sinners would not stumble while ascending to the tomb. Looming over all the hills was Yarmouth Mountain, a graveyard backsliding deceased would do well to avoid. Several graveyards offered scenic vistas: Fair, Park, Sea, Bay, and Lake View, something always worth pondering when one purchases a home, particularly a residence one is likely to occupy for a considerable time. South River and Indian Brook gurgled across a plain before flattening into Willowbank, after which they pinched together and tumbled through Riverdale. Undertakers developed choice locations along the waterways, at Brook and River Side. Morticians dammed waterways and sold executive graves at Lakeside. Groves of Elm, Birch, and Pine filled elbows in valleys while Maplewood sprawled over several ridges before slipping out green and level to Woodlawn and Duffin Meadows. On the map I could not find all the cemeteries mentioned in the newspaper. Although I climbed every hill, even Yarmouth Mountain, though I must add I broke this arduous hike by napping in the Garden of Rest, I was unable to locate the Gate of Heaven. Happily I did not waste much time searching for Resurrection. Just after setting out, I realized that Resurrection would not come into being until Judgment Day. Although I visited Cross Roads and Folly Village, I could not find Jawbone Corner. "Oh, that's just up the road from Shank of the Pelvis and down the slope from Titty Knob," Vicki said one evening as we sat on the well cover sipping a Cabernet Sauvignon.

After leaving Sobey's, we drove back to Beaver River, breaking the journey only to stop at Dayton for vegetables, then at the Quick and Tasty for a late lunch. For lunch I ate a bowl of fish chowder and Vicki a grilled cheese sandwich with "ball park" mustard spread on the bread. At home days swung back and forth, like rockers on the chair by the kitchen stove. Mornings and evenings I sat in the chair, moving but not traveling. While we were in the kitchen, Vicki turned on the radio, usually to the CBC, the Canadian Broadcasting Corporation. At night while washing and drying dishes, we listened to classical music. On weekends we heard "Finkelman's '45's'," a batter of pop talk and music. Bland words were the primary ingredient in most shows broadcast during days. Only occasionally did a program rise yeasty into consciousness. Early in July a program of church music awakened associations sweeter than hot cross buns—"Whispering Hope," "Abide with Me," and "The Church in the Wildwood" becoming the egg yolks and melted butter, the currants and cinnamon of a rack of memories.

That day eventide did not fall fast. Seven years ago my father visited Nova Scotia. As I listened to the music, I saw him sitting in the rocking chair, a copy of Rudyard Kipling's *Just So Stories* in his hands, Eliza perched on his lap, Edward leaning on the left arm of the chair, and Francis standing behind the chair looking over the back, red hair tumbling over his forehead. Among songs sung on the program was

"Precious Memories." This past December Vicki's father died. Vicki spent her first summer in Nova Scotia the year she was born, 1953. Until she married me in 1978, she spent practically every summer in Nova Scotia, traveling up with her father in June and returning with him to New Jersey in September. Traces of Vicki's father lingered throughout the house. His typewriter sat on the desk in the study. In the side entry to the kitchen a cableknit sweater and a pair of corduroy trousers hung on pegs. On a shelf lay a Greek sailor's hat, the bill dried and split. On the floor was a pair of leather shoes, size thirteen. Sometimes on cold mornings when grass was wet, I slipped my feet into the shoes, wearing them like clogs.

A person slips out of mind quicker than he does out of house. The only letters Vicki and I received during the summer were sent by the children from camp. The first letter arrived on July 8. Six days earlier I found a camp letter in the Scotch Room, this letter not mailed from Maine but from Pittsburgh, Pennsylvania, on June 8, 1927, and sent to Vicki's father or "His Lordship, Sir E. D. Johnson," as his correspondent "The Lord of the House of Schover," addressed him. As an adult Vicki's father enjoyed the title professor. As a boy his world was grander. "My Lord," the letter began, "Prince of Paflagonia, Grand Regent of Bithynia, Arch-Duke of the Plenopotentiary of Dalmatia, Grand Khan of the Prefeture of Belsonia, August Registrar of the Diocese of Rhaetia, Lordly Maharajah of East Sinythesia, Grand General of the Royal Paflagonia Hussars, and Lord of A Thousand Titles." Vicki's father spent several summers at Camp Merryweather, a boys' camp in Vermont, and the Lord of the House of Schover wrote, saying that he would not be returning to camp. Instead, the Lord recounted, he was going to spend July in Biddeford Pool, Maine, explaining "my mother wishes to see more of me in the summer."

Vicki's father attended St. Paul's School in Concord, New Hampshire. In the study I found a stack of *Alumni Horae*, the St. Paul's alumni magazine. Each issue began with a letter from the Rector. Two pages long, the letters described school doings, such things as college entrance examinations, the deaths of masters, and ordering commemorative dinner plates from "Messrs. Wedgewood of Stoke-on-Trent." A dozen blue plates cost twelve dollars. Depicted in the center of each plate was a school scene, the Chapel, Lake Penacook, the Upper and

Lower Schools, or Skating on the Pond. Over the border of the plate arbutus bloomed, acorns hung from white oaks, apples ripened, and gray squirrels scurried across boughs of pine. Written in a familiar style, the letters smacked of a time when the benefits of education were clear, a time when educators felt so sure of themselves that they did not hide behind jargon. "The other day I made a sad discovery. I can no longer run up Jerry Hill!" S. S. Drury wrote on October 25, 1927. "Men in their later forties find these limitations irksome. Dependence on eyeglasses, regard for diet, curtailing of tobacco, all obtrude themselves. But it is worth while on an autumn day briskly to walk up Jerry Hill and with any one of you I shall run down without a stop, and then have a nice jog trot through Fergusson Woods, all glistening and swaying with its glorious pines."

Almost never can the eye empty an old house. In past summers I had rummaged the house. This summer I did not think I would discover anything. I was wrong. Nestled amid old clothes in a drawer upstairs was a darning egg. With a black ebony ball attached to one end, the egg resembled a maraca. In order to darn, one pulled a sock over the ball. At the other end of the egg was a silver handle, decorated with scalloped swirls and dots, one design a fern stretching into leaves, another, a minute flower with five petals. In the same drawer I also found a glove stretcher. The stretcher was shaped like a pair of scissors, the two handles made of silver and the blades ivory. Behind the chimney in the pantry I discovered a lemonade pitcher. Decorated with grapes and vines, the pitcher was probably a hundred years old. Three diamonds of grapes hung down the sides of the pitcher. Each diamond contained twenty-four grapes, at the top of the cluster a line of two grapes, immediately below three grapes, below that four grapes, then lines of five, tapering to four, three, two, and finally one grape. In the shed I found a bow saw, eighteen inches tall and twenty-four inches wide at the blade. Wooden spools held the blade in place. Turned sideways, the saw looked like a small harp. I held the saw in my hands and could almost hear it, thrumming, plucking wood chips into melody.

Among the hymns sung on the CBC was "This Is My Father's World." The house was the world of Vicki's father, and memories of him haunted the summer. In comparison to a beloved father, a husband is a cartoon character. Instead of blazing trails through life, people follow examples. Although I do not look like Vicki's father, my life in Nova Scotia resembles his. Vicki's father was a bird watcher. In 1951 he kept a diary. "Most of last summer's friends," he wrote in July, "are back frequenting the same places. Around the house are yellow warblers in great profusion. A pair of redstarts are nesting in the south grove." Thirty-five years later, I, too, watched birds, an activity I began during my first summer in Nova Scotia.

By July most birds had built nests and stopped singing. Some birds were exceptions, however. On foggy mornings a lone song sparrow perched in the willow, music spooling from him like water dripping off the roof. Black-throated green warblers hunted through spruce along the lane, their songs short-circuits of fizzes and sparks. Yellow warblers called from alders. The calls skittered, sounding like marbles shot across a taw and slapping off one another. A pair of catbirds nested at the edge of the woods. My appearance disturbed them, and on noticing me, they shrieked, their cries shriller than those of catbirds in Storrs.

In August groups of chickadees foraged through spruce. Seeming to ignore me, the birds approached within a few inches of my hand. Late in the month mixed flocks of small birds whisked the brush at the edge of the woods: chickadees; black and white, yellow, and myrtle warblers; yellow throats; and red-breasted nuthatches. Often a least flycatcher hung opportunistic on the edge of flocks and pounced on insects stirred out of hiding. Robins appeared so often in the side yard that Vicki dubbed them "lawn chickens."

On many walks I flushed pheasants. In the woods I found two hunting blinds. In both blinds orange twine stretched between two trees. Piled against the twine were fans of limbs. Behind one fan sat a kitchen chair with a white plastic seat while behind the other rested a fish box. The blinds faced stretches of the woods where I disturbed pheasants. I didn't find shotgun shells near the blinds, though. Actually hunters would probably have enjoyed more success if they had sat on our porch. Early most mornings a cock pheasant fed by the meadowsweet. On being disturbed he ran across the grass, his neck stretched forward, making him seem as awkward as a seabird on land. At the end of the yard he threw himself into flight, feathers streaming dusty about him. Later in mornings a hen and three chicks the size of cantaloupes appeared. Usually they perched on a fallen tree and ate, so far as I could tell, ants and pillbugs, pausing between courses to groom themselves.

In "My Father's World," "creatures" were "everywhere," in "earth and trees" and "skies and seas." Six crows perched on the headland. Below them black ducks dotted the water. Beyond the ducks loons called and dived. Amid stones on the beach willets clacked, trying to distract me from fledglings. In mornings at low tide great black-backed gulls congregated beyond the guzzle at Bartlett's. For the first time I noticed terns on the sand, and I watched them parse the water for fish, dropping into exclamations then abruptly pulling up into question marks. Whenever I walked near fledglings, parent birds swooped overhead, screeching, sounding like rusty screened doors being pulled open then released.

Kingfishers nested on the bluffs near Cape St. Mary. Unlike cormorants, whose quick wingbeats sliced smoothly across sight, kingfishers ripped vision, their scoldings torn and jagged. Off Black Point great blue herons fished tidal pools. The birds moved like puppets, their long bills splinters supported by invisible cords. On calm sunny days the heads of harbor seals stuck out of the water, glistening like smooth round stones. When seals basked on rocks, they resembled runners removed from rocking chairs. Cormorants also basked on the rocks. When the birds spread their wings and faced the sun, they formed a phalanx of ornamental pikes. A marsh hawk glided over the bog behind Black Point. The hawk planed the air slowly, yawing then pulling up, beating its wings four or so times before sliding down toward the heath again.

In August I spent much time at Black Point. I caught red-bellied and garter snakes. One day I walked around the Point to Salmon River. From bogs along banks of the river, humic acid streamed into the bay, staining breaking waves yellow and forming shadows, turning the water dark blue. At low tide I wandered rocks jutting in front of Black Point. Snagged on the rocks was a landfill of trash. From the headland twenty feet above someone had pushed a small tractor. At the foot of the slope part of a motor and an axle lay half-buried and rusting. From boats heading to and from Cape St. Mary fishermen tossed plastic containers. One afternoon I counted nine empty white bottles, each once containing 3.6 liters of Javex-12, a sodium-hypochloride solution used "for general sanitation, disinfecting, bleaching." Judging from the litter on the rocks, fishermen were always thirsty. When not inhaling Sprite or diet cola, they drank milk, 2% partly skimmed being the milk of choice. One fisherman at least was adventurous, for amid the rocks lay two empty containers, each of which once held thirty-two ounces of RICE DREAM. "An Organic Original," RICE DREAM was a "1% Fat, Non-Dairy Beverage" made from brown rice.

In August I sat on the headland at Black Point and watched shore birds: semipalmated plovers, sanderlings, and least sandpipers, the "peeps" rattling among rocks or picking through bales of kelp searching for isopods. Willets shifted through tidal pools, the white bars on their wings stuttering. Here and there dunlins dug for worms, black patches staining their bellies and their heads pale and vacuous. During one high tide thirty-four birds clustered on a muffin-shaped rock, barnacles speckling the side of the rock like sugar. Nineteen of the birds were willets; four, terns; five, ruddy turnstones; and six, whimbrels. Of the shorebirds, whimbrels were the most skittish. Flying low, whimbrels skipped over the water, the tips of their wings seeming to skim along the ocean, holding the birds aloft.

Throughout July cries of merlins rang around the house. A pair nested just beyond the side meadow. During much of the day the female perched in a spruce standing in the rose hedge. Porcupines had girdled the tree, and its limbs were bare. The female fanned her tail in the sun, the white and black feathers resembling molding carved out of air. While the female sunned, the male hunted, tossing himself out of the yard then sweeping back low and fast like a boomerang. He cried loudly on his return, and the female flew out of the tree to meet him and seize the meal. Once she had the prey, the female flew into another spruce and plucked the bird. The male was a good provider and down sifted across the side yard throughout July. Once I watched the female bite the head off a tree swallow then strip feathers from the body as if she were unzipping clothes.

The merlins raised four fledglings, three females and a male. Near the end of July the young left the nest and for a few days lived in the windbreak bordering George's Field. Every morning they gathered on the ridgepole of the barn. They seemed affectionate, pressing together and grooming, even snuggling against each other. I stood beneath the barn and watched them. I saw their first broken flights and hard landings. Once the young could fly, both parents hunted, and throughout days the shriek of falcons pierced the silence like sirens. One afternoon I found a red-winged blackbird on the grass in the side yard. I suspect a young merlin dropped the bird and didn't retrieve it, being too inexperienced to land and take off from the ground. The merlins disappeared in the second week in August, during three days when Vicki and I traveled to Maine to fetch the children.

Vicki and I did not leave the house at night. Two or three evenings Bill Grace dropped by for tea, but aside from Bill, no one visited us. Nights were not lonely, however. After dusk, moths flew arabesques around the front door. By ten o'clock moths bunched in beds or hung about window panes in furry trellises. Sharp-angled carpets, salt-and-pepper loopers, and spear-marked and white-banded blacks clumped against each other in tangrams. Saw-wings, deep yellow euchlaenas, and false crocus geometers bloomed like carpet bedding. Copper underwings swirled nervously, showering orange through the light. In comparison once-married underwings were still as buds, the oranges, whites, and blacks of hind wings pinched by the forewings. White and yellow slant lines clung to wood, their bodies blades of stone broken from statuary, the wheat-colored line on the forewings marking places where water seeped beneath the stone, freezing and chipping the statues into flakes. Although wings of clover loopers were gray and black, their eyes were green, and their antennae, red as stems of brambles in October. From a distance many moths appeared drab. In bright light, however, they blossomed. Yellow veins wound through the forewings of maple loopers. Above the veins banks rose black then rolled out to flats of silver, gray, and red. Names of moths sounded like the names of flower bulbs, and I embroidered imaginary terraces with clandestine darts, many-lined wainscots, fingered and afflicted daggers, Isabella and Virgin tiger moths, apple and blinded sphinxes, the eyespots on the hind wings of this moth bright hollyhocks.

Watching moths bloom kept me up at night, and in August I recognized constellations for the first time, the study of basal lines, marginal shades, and orbicular spots having prepared me for stars. In mid-August Perseids streaked the sky, some of the meteors feathery as long-tailed birds. At night I stood in the lane, the blueberry field behind and George's Field in front of me. In the northwest I recognized Boötes, Corona Borealis, Hercules, Draco, and Ursa Major and Minor. In the northeast Cygnus brooded above the Milky Way, and Pegasus galloped above Pisces. In the southeast Sagittarius cantered in and out of sight. In the southwest Scorpius hovered predatory over the ragged shadows of spruce. Beneath constellations airplanes hurried eastward, flying from Boston and New York toward Paris and London. As I looked at stars and then planes flickering like compact constellations, I wanted my thoughts to fly. Alas, I have never saddled Pegasus or sipped the Hippocrene. After thirty minutes of stargazing, my neck usually ached, and I returned to the house and went to bed.

Although Vicki and I did not imagine going to Paris, we didn't spend every day in Beaver River. In July we went to Yarmouth for the parade celebrating "Seafest," the local summer festival. As in the past we watched the parade from Frost Park across Main Street from the town library. This summer the crowd seemed rough. "I see," a man standing on the curb said, "a bunch of fags coming down the street." In order to give his buddies time to chuckle, he paused before adding, "I mean flags." Fifty-four flags, most Canadian, led the parade. Behind them followed a banner preaching, "Proud Canadians Do Proud Things." Next the mayor of Yarmouth rode past in a white Cadillac convertible with bull horns attached to the hood. Although the mayor smiled and waved, no one clapped.

The Department of Tourism promoted the year as "Year of the Wooden Boat," and a fleet of dories motored along Main Street. Pensioners from Villa Saint Joseph sat on the flat bed of a long truck, cardboard gunnels raised around them. From Tidal View Manor a pod of "Sailing Seniors" cruised past, all wearing sailors' caps. Schools of mermaids rode in sandy rowboats. Below the waist the mermaids wore black except for one green and two gold mermaids. The mermaids were young, and most were pudgy, needing to undergo regimens of years or long-distance running. "I thought mermaids looked better than that," the man on the curb said. "If I hooked one of them, I'd throw her back." Schools of minnows also drifted along the street: the Yarmouth Sailorettes wearing red blouses, white shirts, and sailor hats, and the South Shore Bluenose Majorettes, these last so young they seemed roe.

Wearing a watery dress damp with greenery, a woman trotted past, at her side Ripley, an Irish wolfhound eleven months old. Dressed in top hat and a cut-away, a man rode a penny farthing bicycle, sliding from one side of the street to the other. Vicki and I recognized the man from past summers and smiled. Atop a flat truck the Horseshoe Dancers spun through a Virginia reel, and two men played guitars in the back of a small truck belonging to the Rosedale Fur Farm. Two women marched past, holding a banner reading, "Working Together As A Community." Advertising Party Time Decorations, colored balloons shimmered under a fishnet in the back of a pickup. The truck stopped opposite Town Hall, and after a fishermen reeled in the net, the balloons swam through the air like krill, red and yellow, blue, green, and silver.

Despite the penny farthing and the balloons, the parade wasn't as lively as in the past. No drums thumped, and no bagpipes wailed. Rock and roll blared from a radio in a police car. Instead of lifting spirits, the cacophony undermined mood, much as shipworms eat away wooden pilings. Although a Dalmatian hunkered in a fire truck, no Belgian horses strode by, hair hanging off their necks like ferns. Near the end of the parade a truck pulled a puppet theater built by the Yarmouth Wesleyan Church. Draped above the theater was a banner declaring, "He Lives. Jehovah—Rapha." "What does *Rapha* mean?" Vicki asked. "The Lord knows," I said. At the end of the parade Vicki and I decided to make an afternoon of it, and we ate an early dinner at Pizza Delight. We drank Pepsi colas and shared a Caesar salad and a pizza sprinkled with olives, pepperoni, and mushrooms.

In the last week of July, Vicki and I spent a day at the Western Nova Scotia Exhibition. In past summers when the children were young, we rode the Ferris wheel and bumper cars and bought a bushel of candied apples and a hamper of cotton candy. This summer we ignored the midway and walked straight to Homecrafts. Orange dahlias bigger than sunbursts won best in show. A display of bee balm won best perennial. Bouquets of flowers bloomed on quilts. On one quilt daisies hung over the sides of wicker baskets, four daisies to a basket, all with yellow centers, the petals on the blossoms different colors, lavender, red, blue, and purple.

Vegetable gardens wilted atop platters: Pontiac peas, Red Delight rhubarb, Harris Model parsnips, Cherry Bell radishes, Hook Swiss chard, and Cylindra and Detroit Dark Red beets. Potatoes lay in clumps: Irish Cobbler, Early Rose, Kennebec, Fundy, Green Mountain, Idaho, Home Comfort, Stable, Superior, Warba, and Keswick. I think the aroma of hide, hay, sawdust, and manure sweeter than perfume, and I spent much time in the Beef and Dairy Barn, the Charolais, Herefords, Holsteins, Blondes, Shorthorns, and Black and Red Angus resembling nourishing clods of earth. In the Horse Barn Percherons looked like basalt cliffs glistening with ocean spray. Unfortunately the number of animals exhibited this year was smaller than in the past. The motto of the exhibition was "The EX with the Extras." Since Vicki and I last attended an exhibition, some of my favorite extras, rabbits and chickens, had vanished.

In the arena our neighbor George Hall judged the Best Decorated and Best Working teams of oxen. After the judging, Vicki and I explored the Commercial Building before returning to Beaver River, the well cover, rappie pie, and half a bottle of Cabernet Shiraz. The display of the Yarmouth County Association of United Baptist Churches stood beside those of Singer Sewing Machine and Dauphinée Memorial Art. "One to make your shroud, one to wrap you with words, and one to plunk a rock over your head," Vicki said.

A member of the Hubbard's Point Gospel Hall handed out tracts, most published by the Gospel Messenger in Cleveland, Ohio. I took *White Man Lost* and *Hell. Do You Know The Way?* A blue highway curved like a serpent across the cover of this latter tract, flames resembling larkspur sprouting pink by the roadside. The way to Hell, the tract declared, "Is Easy." "To go anywhere on your own, by land, sea or air, you must know the way. To go to heaven, you must know the way." However, I read, "you do not have to know the way to hell! If you die without Christ as your Savior you will automatically arrive there!" In the other tract a hiker broke his compass. For two days the man wandered aimlessly in "the vast northern woods of Canada." Just as the man gave up hope of escaping the forest, an Indian found him. "White man lost," the Indian exclaimed, after which he led the man "to safety."

"Do you know that God says that the whole human race is *lost?*" the tract asked. "Have you ever had a strong desire to be delivered from going to hell? If not, then you have never realized that *you are lost.*"

Vicki and I left Beaver River so infrequently that we ran little risk of getting lost. Still, if I didn't worry about, as *White Man Lost* put it, my "title" to "the mansions above," I did explore plots below, roaming the graveyard above the salt marshes at Chebogue. Near the ocean, shadows vanish from light and sometimes from life itself. Kneeling on the ground at Chebogue, I read tombstones. The inscriptions cheered me. Like an old hymn, the words appealed to feeling rather than thought. Carved on a stone above the grave of a child was the phrase, "Budded on Earth to Bloom in Heaven." "Jesus," I read, could "make a dying bed feel soft as downy pillows." With the sky a smooth blue palm, cautionary inscriptions lost bite. "How frail is man, how short his breath," I read; "In midst of life exposed to death. / How sad an instance of the truth. / Glows in the fate of this dear youth. / Replete with health today at noon. / By one alas his life is gone."

The carvings purged melancholy from the day, and amid the graves I thought about Slubey Garts and country folk in Carthage, Tennessee, who stumble through my essays. Four books ago I described the doings of fictional characters in Port Maitland. During the past five years, however, the inhabitants of Carthage have spread like kudzu through my writings while Bertha Shifney and her acquaintances in Port Maitland have lain dormant. One spring I heard that a new Baptist minister had come to Port Maitland. Bertha did not like him and told the Chenoweths that "he preached with the cloak of hypocrisy stuck to his teeth like plaque." Since I did not spend that summer in Beaver River, however, I heard nothing more about the preacher. This fall, I suspect, Bertha and Nova Scotia will come to mind and I will hear more about matters in Port Maitland. Be that as it may, though, at Chebogue, I thought about Carthage. Early this summer the *Carthage Courier* sponsored a poetry contest. Loppie Groat called his poem "He Speaks to Me," taking the title from the second verse of "This Is My Father's World." "Fe—Fi—Fo—Fum," the first stanza read; "They come; they come. / Up and down, I hear the possums run, / Barking in an unknown tongue." Entitled "June," Googoo Hooberry's entry won fourth prize. "And on the ground," my favorite verse hymned, "the toad has built its nest, / And now is chirping in the trembling leaves. / The fragrant June with myriad flowers is drest, / And all the hills are covered with golden centipedes. / Creeping among the flower pots and pansies, / Are lowly creatures that the poet fancies, / While high up in the greening trees above, / Earwigs sing their songs of love."

Death often brightens paragraphs devoted to Carthage. Early in June Chamomile Spracklin died. Chamomile enjoyed a long career as a rigorous and systematic drinker. People in Carthage are polite, and instead of saying Chamomile died from a detonated liver, they said he "suffered from a lemon-colored epidermis." "As memento mori of her undying infection," as Loppie Groat expressed it, Chamomile's widow Sunday had a handsome verse engraved on her husband's tombstone, the verse, I should add, being similar to one adorning a stone at Chebogue. "His Soul," the tribute stated, "has now taken its flight / To mansions of Glory above, / To mingle with Angels of Light, / And dwell in the Kingdom of Love." Unfortunately Chamomile's will disappointed Sunday, and she instructed Isom Legg to add a postscript to the tombstone. "P. S.," the addition stated, "Not Gone Before But Lost." "If people want to find Chamomile," Sunday told Isom, "tell them he was last seen strapped to the back of a long-eared animal." Dissatisfaction with leavings did not prevent Slubey Garts from preaching a strong funeral sermon. Slubey warned readers against deathbed repentance. "Don't build the lighthouse when the ship is sinking," he said. "The oak grows from an acorn. The branch sawed off and stuck in the dirt won't root, no matter how many tears you pour on the ground. You have to go on the warpath against sin when you are young. As soon as you step out of the tee-pee, be a brave. Seize the tomahawk of Truth and scalp locks from Wrong and hair from Error."

Camp in Maine ended early in August, and Vicki and I brought the children to Nova Scotia. Because school began in Connecticut on August 28, the children stayed in Beaver River for only a fortnight. Vicki and I come from small families. I am an only child, and Mother and Father died in 1988 and 1990, before the children knew them well enough to remember. The children have one first cousin whom they see every four years. Because they are growing up apart from the anchor of a big family, I want the children to feel the magnet of place.

Consequently I decided they should come to Beaver River, no matter how short the visit. "As soon as they see the house," I said, "memory will bind them to the land."

Although my paths had frayed, flowers soon stitched me into place. Moreover as I wandered field and headland, the commonplace of identity faded. Instead of a teacher, I became an explorer, discovering the familiar. In August the children occasionally accompanied me on walks, and I identified flowers for them, hoping that names would ring like bells and awaken recollection: yarrow, eyebright, beach pea, hedge bindweed, queen of the meadow, knapweed, and ragged fringed orchis.

Naming forced me to look closely at flowers. On fireweed, buds resembled sugar scoops, the lower side curved and pink, the upper spreading, exposing folds of petals. From sundew rose a minute hedge of scepters, each topped by a red ball wrapped in clear liquid. I touched a ball with my index finger. Liquid stuck to my fingertip, and when I pulled my finger away, the liquid stretched into a wand. Along the headland at Black Point, seedheads of goatsbeard turned black and instead of opening wilted, resembling the leathery skulls of long-billed birds. In mornings, pillbugs tumbled out of the seedheads. Sow thistle bloomed amid rocks under the headland, five to seven flowers spinning yellow above each stem. In the bog behind the point, purple fringed orchis blossomed, its fragrance fruity and chilled, reminding me of peaches one day, apples the next. Calopogon grew in the bog. Atop lip petals yellow brushes scrubbed the air; below magenta gathered in a bowl. Gerardia flowered amid cranberries; bells dangled from bog huckleberry, and tangles of juniper hugged the ground, the branches so twisted they seemed to twitch.

Near the house golden elder bloomed, the tree's pale yellow leaves floating soapy in the air, blossoms pressed together in cleansing pads, at the end of each stamen a yellow mop. Great spangled fritillaries and white admirals hung on meadowsweet while wood nymphs clapped across the lane and painted ladies basked on the ground flicking their wings, color rising splintery from their backs. Swamp candles wavered around the edge of George's Field, behind them a row of meadowsweet, then roses and lastly alders green against the stone wall, in the shadows of their leaves swarms of cones. Along the lane at the end of August fall dandelion bloomed, and wedges of golden-rod and whirled wood asters split the blueberry field.

Early in July the lane bristled with meadow fescue, the blue inflorescences shining like steel. Tufts of hairy cap moss grew in the damp. Over spore cases veils draped, ashy white at the bottoms but fiery orange at the tops. Near the end of July long rolls of Timothy burst, the anthers yeasty and lavender, the stigmas frosted with white. Rushes grew in dark files along low stretches of the lane, vigorous and sharp in July but drying and shriveling throughout August. Amid the rose hedge Japanese knotweed bloomed the last week in August, flowers spiraling around twigs in fingers, drawing rings of bees. At the end of July hamlets of Indian pipes curled white and conspicuous in the woods. By mid-August the pipes straightened and flecked with black warped out of sight. Clusters of lichens pulled dead trees out of form and in the process made themselves indistinct. At night lichens absorbed beams from my head lamp and became sharp and beveled. Many spruce in the woods were dead. Bark beetles killed some while others blew over in storms, roots prying up umbrellas of dirt and rock. In boggy spots moss rolled over branches and trees, swallowing them like a sock being pulled over a foot.

Cladonia lichens spread across windfalls. Resembling minute goblets, trays of podetia balanced on roots. On damp mornings moisture curled in the podetia, sparkling like champagne. This summer the woods did not become a mushroom garden, and most mushrooms I saw clung to wood, turning broken trees into trellises: orange nest-caps and witches' butter, brown ear fungus, and chalky white cheese polydore. Lenzites betulina climbed dead trees in scales. Amid hairs on the brackets algae thrived, staining the mushrooms dark green, the color aged and corky, unlike the lively green of the peat mosses on the ground. Along the lane fly agaric bloomed, the cap a scoop of lemon ice cream, the flaky patches of volval remnants shreds of white chocolate. In the woods chanterelles and edible boletus flowered. Near the stone wall four sooty milkcaps flowered. Exuding a smoky aroma, the mushroom seemed a sophisticated night creature, its velvet brown cap lined with snowy gills a cape, its thin brown stalk an elegant cane.

During August I explored tidal pools beyond Bartlett's, something

I had not done before. The pools were rocky, and I wore old tennis shoes. Walkers are easily distracted, and some days putting on the shoes took much time. Above the lip of the beach, mats of seaside bluebells rolled over stones and broken shells. Nearby the pale blossoms of wild mustard danced like spray. Seaside spurge sprawled under the mustard, its leaves paired and pinching the stems tightly. Along the beach stretched a terrace of shells, its surface sharp with dog and channeled whelks, moon snails, and razor clams. On the terrace sun bleached the carapaces of rock crabs and dried deadman's fingers. Sponges clasped blue mussels. In pools mussels seemed prisms, currents of blue, purple, and black refracted from silver, fanning light though the water then eddying away into darkness. On the beach the shells looked like the sky, cirrus clouds drifting across pale blue domes tinged with yellow. Storms threw seaweeds high on the beach where they dried black and brittle. In the weeds lurked eggs of skates and fists of waved whelk eggs, the surfaces of these last ropy and rough as parchment.

Rain rarely bothers a walker. In fact bad weather usually helped me concentrate. On foggy days pastels drifted over Black Point, and dead trees along the edge of the bog clung to the soil, looking like ragged spider webs shrinking in the corners of windows. On sunny days the land was so bright that at times I did not notice my surroundings. When days were so gray that birds were invisible, I was always aware of their presence.

Barnacles frosted rocks around pools. Seaweed splayed over the rocks in combs, most commonly knotted wrack and rockweed, on the blades of which hung streamers of tube weed and pompoms of little seaweed. Crusts and sea lichens stained rocks red and brown while under the water Irish moss shone like purple lusterware. Tufts of coral weed clung to both rocks and shells. Brittle and bony, coral weed was my favorite algae, and often I bent over pools for fifteen minutes watching sunlight tease pink and yellow out of a cluster of weed. Beside pools periwinkles wrote paths across sand. In pools themselves crabs backed into crevices, tortoise shell limpets glued themselves to stones, lugworms pushed castings up through sand, and scuds drifted sideways before sliding away and slipping under stones. While anemones bloomed in crevices, strings of knotted thread hydroids zig-zagged along rocks, the white strands strings pulled from the granite by tides. Occasionally pools contained hunks of fish, often the ragged heads of sea ravens, spines jutting through bones in splinters.

As tidal pools were intriguing small worlds, so at times Nova Scotia seemed a pool, one which Vicki and I did not want to leave. Throughout the summer we discussed moving to Beaver River. "The children," Vicki said, "would be fish out of water." We left Nova Scotia on August 25. At home three cardboard boxes of mail waited for me. Measuring twelve by fifteen by twelve inches, each box once contained a dozen bottles of Majorska Vodka. "Days of wine and sea roses are over," Vicki said, glancing at the mail. "I'll bet you won't think of Nova Scotia for six months." Vicki was wrong. In the mail was a letter from Bertha Shifney, written a week before we left Beaver River. After scolding me for neglecting fictional friends in Port Maitland, Bertha said she spent most of June in bed suffering from "an attack of plumbago in the spine of the back." According to her letter, the new preacher bothered her almost as much as her back.

In July Bertha attended a church social at which the preacher, she recounted, appeared "in his usual state of salubrity." The week before the social Melankton Weagle's best milk cow became impacted. In hopes of saving her Melankton poured a gallon of castor oil down her "gullet." "He would have done better," the preacher stated at the social, "to cast oil upon the waters." Bertha's letter was a tidal pool of phosphorescent gossip. The *Vanguard*, she wrote, interviewed Zilpha Huckleberry on her one hundred and fifth birthday. Only twenty-four, the reporter was young enough, Bertha said, to attend Sunday school. "One hundred and five," he said to Zilpha, a smile as broad as a squash on his face, "and never bedridden." "What do you mean never been ridden?" Zilpha exclaimed. "I've been ridden thousands of times, in the barn, in the pasture, on a bench in front of the courthouse, in the vestry of the church. I've been rid pretty near anywhere a body can be rid, and I've enjoyed every gallop." Before the reporter could speak, Zilpha opened the front door. "Never been ridden!" she exclaimed. "What do you take me for—some sort of spindle-assed town girl? I've never been so insulted. Get out of my house." "Vicki," I said that night at dinner, "I think we'll go back to Beaver River next summer."

October

$\mathcal{L}$ife is genial in spring and summer. Days lengthen then stretch lazily, and the ends of things seem distant. In winter, death resembles a cousin far beyond the pale of familiarity. Mind probes under the snow and discovers a world greening with possibility. Like a bud swelling in warm rain, mind sucks the appointments of fecund dream from season and imagines leaf and bloom. In October, alas, as days shorten and leaves dry yellow and orange, thoughts of loss numb enjoyment and slice into happiness like slivers of night. Every day I swim in the university pool. Only in the fall do I pay attention to people in adjoining lanes. Most swimmers are young, and in comparison to them, sliding silver through the water like translucent leaves clapping in an April breeze, I seem brown and withered. So that I would not become melancholy and ponder the final spectral raking, this fall I swam beside the oldest person in the pool. Every six lengths I lapped her, creating the illusion that I was still green, if not with chlorophyll, at least with a rooty, wintry vigor.

Illusions are dangerous. Instead of turning through laps like a quiet backwater, I swirled, even flipping over and jerking myself into backstrokes. In the middle of September I splashed against the end of the pool like a breaking wave, whacking the back of my head. Shortly thereafter, pain started eddying across my head. As headaches oozed over my skull like water absorbed by cardboard, pain drained energy and dried joy. "My borrowed earth is being recalled," I told Vicki. At night I studied my balance sheet, calculating assets, both the funds I would leave to Vicki and the children and fun I had enjoyed for half a century. For a wall of mud, I'd held up well. After seven weeks, a doctor ran my skull through an MRI machine. He discovered nothing amiss, and though pain nipped at pleasure for three more weeks, no longer did headaches blast dream and winter out of mind.

In October, however, I struggled to purge concern for my head out of head. Often I walked in woods to distract myself from self. At times walks seemed feverish, resembling leaves red and clotted with sugar. As I arranged assets of property and insurance in clear columns so I imagined neatening wood and field, an impossibility in October when endless shucks of leaves scratch air and ground. In past years I celebrated the disorder of fall, describing changes not as ends but as beginnings, the stuff of fertility and creation. Then neatness seemed the cousin of sterility. Imposing order on hill and field, on days themselves, not only blasted possibility but reduced spangled season to just another lump of time. Despite the "abdominal headaches," as my fictional friend Loppie Groat labeled them, my mood eventually changed, however. Rarely does anything that occurs in the classroom influence me. Still, late in October an essay handed in by a freshman made me realize that order is a fiction. No matter how one struggles to neaten life on paper, lively error always smudges the page.

In the essay the student analyzed her reaction to a movie. Before handing me the paper, she ran it through the spell checker on her computer. Spell checkers flag misspelled words, but they do not catch typing errors that transform one word into another word. My student meant to write a dull, functional sentence, stating, "my tears of happiness soon became tears of sadness." Instead her sentence was quick with disorderly error, declaring, "my tears of happiness soon became teats of sadness." "That reminds me of something that happened at the Tabernacle of Love," Hoben Donkin said after I described the girl's error. Last week Abigail, Leviticus Tuttle's milk cow, wandered away from Goose Creek. Leviticus asked Slubey Garts to describe the cow in church, saying Abigail would be easy to recognize because, as he put it, "her rump's done prolapsed and one of her tits is plugged." "Leviticus is as deaf as an alabaster tombstone," Hoben said, explaining that a mistake occurred on Sunday. Before taking up collection Slubey announced the engagement of Flossie Cahoon. When Slubey praised the virtues of the bride-to-be, Leviticus thought Slubey was describing Abigail. When Slubey called Flossie, "the flower of Christian womanhood through whose bosom kindness flows like milk," Leviticus interrupted shouting, "Amen brother. That's right, but don't forget to tell folks about her sour titty."

In the woods fallen trees resembled coffins, shrouds of birch leaves sagging yellow over them and mourning bands of fungus running green through seams in the bark. From the trees artist's fungus and orange stump mushrooms stuck out in handles while knobs of puffballs clustered together like carved decorations. Although sprigs of small blue and white asters lingered here and there, mushrooms, not flowers, blossomed at the end of summer: dumpy blewits, gills and stalks lavender, the caps purple around the edges but bruised and browning in the centers; the deceiver, *laccaria laccata*, hot and copper-red, but cooling pale through the month; and poisonous, dessert-sized earthballs, outsides chips of caramel, underneath white mint melted around lumps of dark bitter-sweet chocolate. Mood affected my vision. Young white pines growing in the raspberry field appeared bedraggled, needles at the tips of branches green cuffs, the sleeves behind, however, fraying, the needles drying yellow and brittle before breaking in the wind, leaving limbs bare and as fragile as old men's arms. As I looked at the pines, a hawk flew over the field whistling, the sound no longer jaunty with spring but misty and mournful, instead of expanding like a bud in sunlight, shrinking to cold white bone.

In October granite boulders became noticeable, turning woods into battered graveyards, the boulders themselves toppled tombstones, rolled out of rectangles and horseshoes, then sunk in the ground. For me graveyards are happy places. When I saw the stones, I thought about my favorite graveyard, the Pillow of Heaven Cemetery in Carthage, Tennessee. October rumpled the Pillow. Early in the month Adipose McClarin died from a wasting disease. Shortly afterward one of Hink Ruunt's wives died. Although I not only sired Hink but gave birth to him and his extensive domestic history, I'm not sure what number wife died. In my books Hink's matrimonial doings have gotten out of hand, and the only thing that might stop him from prancing up to the altar three or four times a year would be an accident to me, say the Hearse of Time's careening off Route 195 and onto the sidewalk, flattening me while I was zipping around Storrs on my bicycle. Be that eventuality as it may, however, Hink's wife was a Boguski from Maggart. She died suddenly, and her family paid for engraving her tombstone. "Hungry Death devoured her without warning," the stone recounted. "She was well at night and dead at nine in the morning."

October was hard on the Boguskis. Just before Halloween, Pony Boguski drowned in the Cumberland River. Having spent much of October visiting relatives in Kentucky, Hoben Donkin returned to Carthage just as Pony's casket was carried into the Tabernacle of Love. "Whose funeral is this?" Hoben asked Googoo Hooberry. "Pony Boguski," Googoo answered. "Good Lord!" Hoben exclaimed, "did he die?" "Well, if he didn't," Googoo said, using his tongue like a peavey to roll a toothpick from the right side of his mouth to the left, "somebody's playing a mighty rough trick on him."

A drunk and a miser, Pony wasn't much loss. "The only time Pony ever visited a doctor," Turlow Gutheridge said, "was after he dropped a pint of whiskey on the floor. Most of the whiskey sloshed out of the bottle, and Pony had to get Dr. Sollows to remove splinters from his tongue." Niggardliness caused Pony's death. A storm washed away the bridge that crossed the Cumberland near Rome. Until a new bridge was completed, travelers were forced to use a private ferry to cross the river, the price of a round trip being ten cents. Too tight to pay the fee, Pony tried to swim the river, even though he had never learned to swim. "By the high waters he was confounded," the verse on his tombstone explained. "He couldn't swim, so he drownded."

I wasn't the only person suffering from vapors in October. Morris Hamper, the wealthiest man in Carthage, caught the croup. On meeting Morris outside the Walton Hotel, Loppie Groat prescribed a vacation. "Morris," he advised, "a couple of weeks in Maggart will set you up nicely. In living memory not a single rich man has died in Maggart." Improbable as it seems, Morris followed Loppie's suggestion and rented a room in Tattle's Boarding House. Sometime later Hoben Donkin met Loppie at the soda fountain in Read's Drugstore. "How's Morris doing?" Hoben said; "I haven't seen him around for a while." "Oh, he's much better," Loppie said. "He's been down in the country for seven days in order to regain his strength." "That's funny," Hoben said, pausing and rubbing the index finger of his right hand along the underside of the little finger on his left hand, "that's odd. I would have reckoned that seven days in the country would have made one weak."

Throughout October Hoben was cheery, particularly about other people's ailments. One morning he met Isom Legg coming out of Dr. Sollows's office. "Isom," Hoben said heartily, "how are you doing?" "Not so well, Hoben," Isom responded. "I suffer terribly from glaucoma and the galloping diabetes. My ears itch. My sleeping trumpet is plugged, and I'm on my way now to buy a truss for my rupture." For a moment Hoben paused, his brow as furrowed as a jigsaw puzzle. But then words slipped into place, and he spoke. "Rupture, smupture, bowlegged, tealegged bumpture," he said, "what do such things matter so long as you are healthy?" Behind Hoben's ebullience percolated the success of the Patent Greens Company, an eatery that Hoben opened in the basement of the Walton Hotel.

Meals were simple and cheap, and the menu listed fried chicken, corn soup, sweet potatoes, okra, and black-eyed peas, these last usually in hoppin John, combined with rice and salt pork. Hoben's specialty, however, was turnip greens cooked with hog jowl and served with cornbread and pitchers of flaky, yellow buttermilk. Almost as popular as greens were pole beans or snaps, the Kentucky Wonder variety, cooked with pieces of ham hock. The success of the restaurant surprised not only Carthage but also Hoben. At first Hoben called the restaurant Greens. Once he made a little money, though, he worried that someone might steal his idea. As a result he decided to patent the restaurant, and he hired Isom Legg to paint "Patent Greens Company" on a white board, which he nailed above the stairs leading down into the basement of the hotel.

Hoben's success spawned offspring, and his cousins in southern Kentucky opened branches of the restaurant in Summer Shade, Zula, and Flippin. Small doings have large consequences. No trace of the Company remains today, but unlike the philosophic tree that forever tumbles silently in the forest because no one is present to hear it slam onto the ground, the effect of the Company reverberates though the restaurant industry today. Years ago while traveling near the Tennessee state line, Colonel Sanders, the founder of Kentucky Fried Chicken, dined at the three restaurants owned by Hoben's relatives. "Out of those helpings of greens crawled," wrote Ursula O. Ingram of the Wharton School of Business, "the worm of inspiration. For years the worm dozed in the Colonel's mind, but then one spring it broke its chrysalis and fluttered brightly across the economy as genus Franchise, species KFC, or the fast food butterfly, as it has been dubbed by learned colleagues at the Harvard School of Business."

Hoben was not alone in celebrating the expansive, entrepreneurial aspects of October. The last week in the month I received a letter from Mrs. Neeoscaleeta Pemberton, Fundraising Secretary of the "Carts For Wienie Dogs Foundation," a society which purchases wagons for crippled dachshunds. An old friend, Mrs. Pemberton writes me every two or three years. Like tombstones in the Pillow of Heaven Cemetery, her letters banish dark thoughts and soothe headaches.

In October Mrs. Pemberton wrote me as Chair of the Billy Bob Costumes For Wienie Dogs on Carts Subcommittee or the BBCFWDOCS, as she put it. Stapled to the upper left corner of Mrs. Pemberton's letter was an advertisement depicting Billy Bob, a Scotty, wearing country dress: blue jeans, a wide black belt, a red checkered shirt with red plastic buttons, and then around the dog's neck a red and white handkerchief. "Watch your dog take on a new PERSONality when he dresses in his people-like jeans and shirt. A novelty outfit for those special events when ordinary doggie threads just won't do," declared an advertisement beside the picture. "Hand washable" and priced at $17.99, the threads came in three sizes: small for dogs weighing up to twenty pounds, medium for dogs ranging between twenty-five and forty-five pounds, and large, suitable for dogs between forty-five and seventy-five pounds. A size for "hefty" or "full-figured" canines was not yet available.

"Dear Friend of Wienie Dogs," Mrs. Pemberton wrote in her letter, "Your generosity has made it possible for wienie dogs, regardless of their financial situation, to seize the opportunity to have a cart for their daily use. But as Halloween approaches, we are making a special plea for assistance. While your own festively attired dog romps through your neighborhood, collecting treats and soaping windows, there will be hundreds of wienie dogs on carts across the country staying at home for lack of a costume, naked and without hope. It doesn't have to be that way, however. Through a pledge to our Halloween costumes for wienie dogs on carts fund drive, you can make a difference. Your gift of $17.99 will purchase a Billy Bob outfit for a needy wienie dog. Just think what $35.98 would do. We are counting on you. Remember, the opportunity to provide a Halloween costume for a wienie dog on a cart is a terrible thing to waste." To the end of her letter, Mrs. Pemberton attached a postscript, asking if I had considered including the Carts For Wienie Dogs Foundation in my "will or estate plans." For details she listed a telephone number and instructed me to "ask to speak to Eldredge B. 'Bud' Smarr."

Walking in woods in summer is difficult. Saplings become throws of leaves, and limbs switch, ready to startle and snare. In contrast, October opens woods and reduces undergrowth to twigs. Slipping down hillsides and across creeks in October, the eye rarely snags on a branch and vision does not weep and blear. In the open woods the walker looks and thinks past the immediate. As I squinted in hopes of thrusting sight over a ridge, I realized how fragmentary was my knowledge of nature, how limited my awareness, even of such a petty matter as writing. In October I read "The Fight," an account of a boxing match written by William Hazlitt in 1822. Hazlitt's essay has been called the "best piece of sports writing in English." In the essay Hazlitt described not simply "the battle" itself but his journeys to and from the ring in Hungerford, England. Hazlitt labeled aficionados of boxing lovers of "the FANCY." In the essay Hazlitt celebrated both the "Fancy" bound by a ring and that uncircumscribed Fancy, the imagination, as people and ideas sparred and parried wondrously through rounds of paragraphs.

In October the women's soccer team at the university was ranked second in the nation. After reading "The Fight," I sauntered over Golf Hill to watch the team play Rutgers. I took a pad and pencil with me to the game, thinking if I could not write "The Fight" I might clap "A Struggle" together. I failed. Unlike Hazlitt I was unable to appoint the afternoon with character and meaning. As the game bounced over the field, I counted the number of portable toilets east of the stadium. There were eight toilets, all with green doors. In fact I counted four times to insure my reckoning was accurate. Later I studied the hairdos of girls playing for the university. Although the goalie knotted her hair into a bun, the other ten girls wore pony tails. A fortnight later I tried once more to transform myself into a sportswriter. This time I attended a football game between teams from the university and from Hofstra. Because the day was cold, I did not sit in the shade with people who cheered for Connecticut. Instead I sat in the sun on the opposite side of the field among a crowd of Hofstra supporters. Again I carried paper and pencil with me. Instead of paraphernalia for writing, the Hofstra supporters brought cardboard placards eighteen inches tall and two feet wide. Across the placards stretched three bands of color, yellow at the top, blue at the bottom, and in the middle white on which were stamped blue letters spelling *Hofstra*. I listened to conversations and jotted down remarks. I heard nothing fanciful. When a tackle blocked a punt, the man sitting in front of me said, "There's a hero in the dorm tonight." Before a kick-off a woman yelled, "Run it back, eighty-eight!" At the beginning of the second half, several people shouted, "Let's go, guys!" Toward the end of the game people chanted, "Go D," the *D* standing for defense. "Did you get some good material?" Edward asked that night at dinner. "Yes," I said, "life resembles an extra point." "How?" Edward asked. "I don't know. I'm not a philosopher," I said, getting up from the table and leaving the kitchen.

Several faculty members besides me swim in the university pool. One day near the end of October my friend Chuck and I finished swimming at the same time. As we stood in the shower, Chuck scrubbing his parts and I rubbing a shampoo fragrant with artificial coconut through my hair, we talked about nature writing. Did I, Chuck wondered, find "spirituality" in Nature? No, I explained, I was not a philosopher. "I'm not able," I said, rinsing suds out of my eyes, "to transcend the particulars of moment." What I did not say was that I found particulars themselves wondrously satisfying and that the search for insight often blurred vision, obscuring not merely the fine clarity of moment but also the capacity to appreciate ordinary life.

I saw many soccer games in October. Edward played fullback on the middle school team and Eliza sweeper on the town travel team. For me, the best moment occurred just after one game. On this particular afternoon both the middle school girls' and boys' teams played at the school, the girls on the upper field and the boys on the lower. Their battle having ended before that of the boys, the girls stood on the sideline and cheered their classmates. When time ran out, the girls gamboled onto the field to congratulate the boys. Two boys strode toward the girls, but the rest scampered away toward the opposite sideline. There they circled in a clot, no one detaching himself from his fellows. Only when the girls approached the sideline did the clot shatter into corpuscles, most of the boys, including Edward, jumping over a wooden bench and drifting hurriedly onto the softball field. For a few seconds the girls milled about before the bench, but then suddenly they turned and, running back toward the school, climbed the steep slope above the playing field. At the top they stopped and, turning around, lay down like logs along the lip of the slope. Once the whole team was stretched out, they rolled down the hill giggling. "I used to do that," Susan said, "but after a boy asked me to go to a movie, I became self-conscious and stopped."

By the end of October I stopped wrestling with Fancy. The headaches lessened, and I spent more time wandering hill and pasture. One morning I got up at dawn. Around the edges of fields, bittersweet splattered trees like batter. Below the sheep barn, oak leaves stained the ground cordovan. Near the Fenton River, morning light sifted dusty through hemlocks. Beneath hemlocks stretched a parquet floor of tan needles. Along the riverbank itself cords of roots bound trees to earth. Often trunks bowed over the water then swept upward in curves, the heavy wood billowing lightly like canvas. Oddly, as trees lost leaves and shrank into sticks, I noticed them more than in summer. Swarms of cones floated at the top of a birch almost as if a net had caught on branches and then been tossed into knots by winds. A thicket of euonymus sprayed out over an old road. Much as years had worn the road out of lane and shoulder, so season washed definition from leaves, turning them ghostly pink. On beeches leaves glowed. Bronze and orange with yellow tippling along veins, the leaves resembled ancient paper, the surface absorbing light and massaging thought into repose and understatement.

Near the hut atop ski-tow hill I sat on the ground. A woolly bear caterpillar bumped through grass, the tufts of hair on its back shining as if they had been dipped in lacquer. A blue jay clattered in the woods, and a downy woodpecker jabbed sprays of poison ivy. I stood and started down the hill. A small flock of cedar waxwings swept out of a hawthorn, and robins snapped into the air, their cries tight as wire. Along the hill, brushes of cypress spurge lay on the ground. The leaves bristled, and when I combed my hand through them, they sloughed off in waves. I looked into the distance and noticed a great horned owl perched in an oak, resembling a Staffordshire bird on a mantelpiece. Wild leek grew at the bottom of the hill, and in the sunlight its seeds shone like gun metal. At the edge of the Beaver Pond grapevines snaked through trees. Clusters of grapes shriveled on the vines, looking like damp bags drying into wrinkles.

October seems to affect student essays, no matter the area of the country. A friend wrote from Alabama and quoted an essay in which a student said she pitied people "afflicted with the Catholic faith." Suddenly I found myself in Carthage, not in a graveyard this time but in a doctor's office, prescribing a remedy for someone else's throbbing head. Every three or four years an epidemic of religious ailments swept through the malarial hollows around Carthage. A revival usually being the source of the contagion, Dr. Sollows doused the feverish with common sense, prescribing a theological diet lean on testifying and hymn singing. Occasionally, though, a patient suffered from symptoms that threatened to burst the girdle of the good doctor's patience. In October Piety Goforth became convinced he was "afflicted with the Catholic faith," notwithstanding his never having been exposed to a Catholic dead or alive.

An unholy litany of symptoms plagued Piety. Late at night Piety felt weak at the knees and heard bells. Some mornings dressing was difficult because he wanted to wear his bathrobe all day and lounge around the house, looking like, he explained, "the big fellow in Rome." Even worse, rain frightened him because he thought it tasted like holy water. Moreover, a recent trip to the stockyards had given him "the yips." "When I shooed flies away from my face," he said, "I moved my hand from left to right and then up and down and made a Romanist sign."

Because Piety's symptoms were various, Dr. Sollows took the patent medicine approach and blended an assortment of cure-alls in his prescription. He instructed Piety to drink a cup of pink tea every morning at breakfast and to sleep with a bible under his pillow at night. For a month Piety was to say three obstreperous Hallelujahs at church on Sunday. Additionally the doctor gave Piety two medicines: Elephant

Pills, an inexpensive flour and paste placebo, which he told Piety to swallow by the "trunkful," and then, for those occasions when bells disturbed Piety's peace of mind, "a bowel freshener of the first rank," concocted from a mixture of senna, may apples, asparagus, and castor oil. The explosion resulting from a dose of the freshener would, the doctor assured Piety, overwhelm the sound of the bells. Finally, Dr. Sollows urged Piety to stay away from drink, observing that Piety did not get his red nose from sipping water colors and warning him that if he tried to drown his worries in spirits the worries might become expert swimmers. "That prescription would probably cure toothache and tight shoes and make a first-class pickler besides being a substitute for turpentine," my friend Josh said in November, before asking if Piety recovered from his affliction. "Certainly," I said, adding that "writing the prescription bucked me up. After I wrote it, my headaches vanished completely."

Messing About

$\mathcal{A}$t the beginning of Kenneth Grahame's *The Wind in the Willows*, Water Rat said to his friend Mole, "there is *nothing*—absolutely nothing—half so much worth doing as simply messing about in boats." Instead of sculling through experience in hopes of exploring new psychological lands, the animals played. In contrast, Huck Finn sailed down the Mississippi River with Jim, the runaway slave. Rather than traveling north, Huck headed south into the frightening world of slavery. The trip tested Huck and Jim, and the journey became a progress heavy with significance. When Mole and Ratty went on a picnic, they stayed near home. When Mole upset the boat in his eagerness to row, nothing profound was meant. Wildly happy and excited as a child with a new toy, Mole just lost control of the oars.

I have reached the stage of life in which I agree with Ratty. Nothing seems half so much worth doing as messing about. Indeed I think Hell to be a place where everything matters, a world where belief so shackles people to purpose that they spend their lives bent like slaves in the hot sun, chopping and hoeing action into significance, so ginning events that they force others into peonage, transforming them into moral and intellectual sharecroppers.

When I was young, mathematics seemed to reflect life itself. I thought hard work would enable both individuals and societies to solve problems. Much as a geometrical theorem could be proved, so truth existed. The study of mathematics created the illusion of order. Below the chaotic surface of things lay not only axioms and postulates, theorems as regular as equilateral triangles, but reason itself. Nowadays instead of mirroring life, mathematics seems matter for a sideshow at a county fair: swimming in a tank, a fish-eating calculus; a trigonometry, cloudy in a bottle of formaldehyde; and on a shelf stuffed, a spotted algebra, one of its linear equations purple, the other orange. Unlike finite mathematics variable English now seems to reflect life. Not only is language a chaos of idiom and definition, but rules of speech and grammar seem more whim than law, reducing the attempt to write "good" English to linguistic messing about. Completing the square may solve quadratic equations, but parsing sentences will not explain the workings of good prose. The real roots of fine writing lie outside formulaic scratchings.

Over the years beliefs and proofs I once thought truths have unraveled like the snail whose body peels into slime as he crawls. When Mole tumbled out of the boat, Ratty rescued him, grabbing him behind the neck and pulling him to the surface. Meaning didn't accompany Mole's return to land. Wet, not reborn, Mole did not push off into pools of significance, and smiting the tinkling current, seek "a newer world." Instead, he went home, and putting on slippers and a dressing gown, sat by the fire with Ratty. As snails crawl through time out of existence, they leave behind glistening trails. The trails are shallow; yet I enjoy seeing them wrap the ground in silver ribbons. I have grown comfortable with surfaces. Actually I think only fictions lie beneath appearances, delusions forced upon picnickers and swimmers by narrow overseers intent upon cultivating crops of meaning.

Much as rats don't associate with poor farmers, so critics leave me alone with the superficial, preferring instead to mine trails of significance which they imagine lurk golden under sentences. Everything is fleeting, of course, particularly meaning. Coker Knox, speaker of the Tennessee House of Representatives, traveled to Carthage last week to dedicate the Horton Sevier State Park. Half brother of John Sevier, one of the founders of Tennessee, Horton Sevier made a fortune trading with Indians. For a hundred years or as long as histories of Tennessee have been manufactured, scholars believed Horton's trading post was located near Castalian Springs in Sumner County. Six years ago, however, while searching for Jeddry, his mule, Loppie Groat discovered a mound in the woods behind Battery Hill. Thinking he had stumbled upon Bluebeard's treasure, Loppie returned at night and opened the mound. Instead of chests glittering with pieces of eight, he unearthed a handful of beads, two buckets of shards, and the rusty barrel of a long rifle. Since money was not involved, Loppie described the mound to the crowd at Ankerrow's Café. Not long afterward the University of Tennessee at Martin sponsored a dig, and students uncovered the foundation of "Sevier's Fort." This past spring the Tennessee legislature passed a bill establishing the park. History, Coker Knox declared in his dedicatory address, "is magical. Only ten years ago the spot where we now stand was located somewhere else." Most historical magic depends on sleight of mind. Forever being revised, the only permanent thing in history is impermanence.

My friend Josh delights in whetting his tomahawk on the skulls of historians. "In one generation the Indian of my childhood, gloriously red in paint and knife, has lost his way, going from the warpath to the sawdust trail, becoming so sanctified that if Jesus were to appear tomorrow historians would bundle him into a sweat hut and make him atone for the sins of whiteness before they would condescend to palaver about the Resurrection." "The historical Indian is so saintly," Josh continued, slicing deep into his subject, "that it's a wonder that when our ancestors arrived in the New World they didn't immediately fall on their knees and beg to be eviscerated." "Maybe, though," Josh said, pausing, "they were selfless and endured the hardship of life so their descendants could partake of the higher pleasure of being skinned alive in tribal casinos."

Josh bathes in streams a little too hot for my tepid taste. Still, neverending interpretation undercuts history, turning truth into trinket, the ripples of event no more significant than those caused by Mole's tumbling into the river. According to Josh, intellectual incubation in this country lasts fifty years. "By the time people hatch," Josh told me, "they have slept so long in the nest their brains are addled." Josh may be right. Only when I emerged from chickenhood at middle age did I stop genuflecting before the brow of history.

Age teaches a person to avoid believers. Wooden cheese and leather ham satisfy most people, even the converted, and when confronted by social evangelicals, one keeps them at idea's length by serving the prefabricated words they hunger to hear. Occasionally a

Pentecostal wants to masticate more than Eukanuba. Not so flexible as folks who mess about, believers are easily duped, however. When rustlers raided farms above Carthage, Ben Meadows shot holes in the side of his cattle barn. Around the holes he drew bull's-eyes. Each hole rested in the center of a bull's-eye, making the rustlers think Ben a dead shot. Although thieves stole cattle from every farm bordering his land, Ben didn't lose a calf.

Instead of planning hours, I mess about. Generally something interesting occurs. Plans sire frustration and boredom. Like Ratty's rowboat, plans invariably go belly up, dumping their originators into cold water. So that he could adjust chores to fit his feelings, last month Piety Goforth bought a mood ring from a peddler. "Piety would have done better to have grabbed a feather duster or a zinc-fluted washboard for all the good that ring done him," Googoo Hooberry said. "Piety forgot he was color-blind, and the next morning when he studied the ring, he couldn't see green or red, nor even blue. He just saw brown, so he shoveled manure all day." Rarely do people plan for eventualities. When fleas infested her house, Clevanna Farquarhson cinched flea collars around her ankles. "That's the most short-sighted thing I've ever heard," Clevanna's cousin Loppie Groat said later. "What's going to happen when she has to walk on her hands?"

While expectation inevitably brings disappointment, messing about leads to surprise. When Hink Ruunt's mare Centauress got caught in a barbed wire fence and ripped off four-fifths of her tail, Hink bought a jar of Growing Salve from Daddy Snakelegs, a faith doctor. Hink rubbed the salve into the remains of Centauress's tail, and the salve worked, but not quite as Hink expected. The nub sprouted and budded, not into bushy tail, but into another horse, a white stallion. Instead of a single mare, Hink now owned a team of horses joined backside to backside. A flexible and creative entrepreneur, Hink has always been able to squeeze coin out of difficulty. When Centauress came into heat, goings-on in Hink's barn were astonishing, so much so that Hink arranged dining-room chairs around Centauress's stall and charged admission. Although Hink made money, the real beneficiary of his planning was Dr. Sollows, who refused to attend a single show, even when Hink offered him a complimentary ticket. For two weeks after each estrus, the good, curious citizens of Carthage besieged

Dr. Sollows, complaining of bruised withers, twisted gaskins, premature fetlocks, and detumescent pasterns. Last spring a bit lodged in Vardis Grawling's throat, and Dr. Sollows extracted it with obstetrical forceps.

No one is immune to the spirit of an age. Despite knowing that plans can only go awry, I organize days for the children. In summer I send Eliza to camp in Maine in hopes she will learn to pull a bow and build a fire. I want her to handle a canoe better than Mole so that she will be able to paddle south and journey out into whatever Mississippi's appeal to her. I also send her so that she will brush against girls who live in places wider than our backwater. Two weeks ago, Vicki, the children, and I discussed words at dinner. As usual I stressed the arbitrary nature of language. I pointed out differences between meanings of the same word in English spoken in the United States and in English spoken in Great Britain. "In London," I said, *"fanny* does not mean bottom. It's slang for a female's private parts." Before I could continue, Eliza broke in excitedly, shouting, "so is *pussy!*" Silence erupted. The boys stared at the tablecloth, and Vicki's fork sagged, spilling a hunk of pineapple on the linoleum. After my chair settled, I asked Eliza where she got her linguistic knowledge. "On the school bus?" I asked. "No," Eliza said, "at camp. I learned lots of neat things there." "Four thousand, two hundred and fifty dollars," I said to Vicki later, "and Eliza learns the p-word." "What did you expect?" Vicki asked rhetorically. "That she'd learn to swim? Don't be naive."

The child of the snake isn't taught to bite. As I age, I have come to think that behavior is determined more by genes than anything else, except perhaps luck. Instead of a camp follower, Eliza is an offshoot of my DNA. Her use of strong language did not startle me. In greener days when the concept of free will seemed almost plausible, before family evolved into one wife, two dogs, and three children, I used strong words. Language has always delighted me, as it did my mother, and if I had known what *fanny* meant in British slang, the cancan would have occasionally bounced low-stepping across my conversation, so to speak.

When a teacher attributes his success to education, no one except other teachers believes him. In a world in which genes, not school, shape adults and in which messing about contributes as much to achievement as planning, education often seems more indulgent than beneficial. Because the ivied platitudes that once buttressed education have crumbled, Josh said recently, "universities choose boosters as presidents, jumped-up Rotarians who can't distinguish a penwiper from a post-hole digger. Forty years ago," he continued, spurning the peace pipe when I tried to interrupt him, "such people accomplished things in small towns, sponsoring spaghetti suppers at high schools and running bake sales on behalf of local hospitals. Nowadays university bureaucrats plaster faults in the mock gothic with butt-sprung words like *excellence* and *commitment*. Then before people notice the whole educational fabric shaking from intellectual palsy, administrators rhapsodize about athletics."

Although generally a man to my tooth, Josh can be zealous. He ought to mess about more. He needs to relax and enjoy athletics, and, for that matter, education. Instead of demanding that education benefit society, he just ought to enjoy the spectacle. This semester, I, for example, dallied, if not along a riverbank, at least in bleachers far from classrooms, seeing eight girls' soccer games, one boys' soccer game, three football games, two volleyball games, a swim meet, and a field hockey game. To be truthful I attended in part in order to sun myself. Age has made me cold-blooded, and if I don't absorb enough heat before writing, my prose freezes sharp and biting. "Huh!" Josh, grunted, "bleat with faculty one minute. Then roar with trustees the next. What sort of man are you?" "A happy one," I replied, "a man who thinks there is nothing half so worth doing as messing about." "Butting the times causes headaches," I added; "nothing lasts. Both foolishness and wisdom vanish in an hour." I ended my sermonette by quoting an engraving I saw on a tombstone in the Pillow of Heaven Cemetery in Carthage. "The Body born of Clay, / Blooms in a Night, / And withers in a Day."

The compulsion to find meaning distorts vision and undermines possibility. In November I attended an exhibition of Tiffany lamps held in the art museum at the university. People ought to consider art toys, like Ratty's boat and sculls, rather than propaganda or cultural icons. Insignificance is a fine conservator. Instead, say, of anger or disgust, insignificant art awakens the healthiest and most straightforward and protective reaction: covetousness. Rather than interpreting a piece of art out of identity, the person who covets wants the art itself. At the exhibition I coveted a ninety-year-old "Wisteria Table Lamp." Over the open crown of the shade, leading twisted in hard, dark branches. Soft, blue clumps of wisteria fell down the border of the shade while from the base of the lamp roots swirled outward in a skirt. In imagination I set the lamp atop the dowry chest in the living room. I dreamed of dozing beside the lamp on cold evenings. While snow shook like filigree though the street lamp outside, inside blue petals twinkled like rain. I stared at the lamp for a long time, moving only when a stranger wearing a deerstalker cap spoke to me. "Tiffany was something else," the man said. "He didn't have an insane bone or organ in his body, not even an insane pancreas." Folks who mess about are loners, wary of entanglement, slipping easily from one activity to another. When strangers approach, words curling oddly over their lips, people who mess about behave like Vardis Grawling when Loppie Groat showed her a green snake he plucked from a lilac bush. "Don't be afraid, Vardis," Loppie said; "it's only a green snake." "Yes," Vardis answered, picking up her skirt and stepping backward, "but it might be as dangerous as a ripe one."

This fall I rummaged about in the basement of the library. Entombed there are books that have not been checked out in decades. In the basement I dug through mounds of natural history books, occasionally uncovering glittering artifacts. How nice to know that larvae of the gold-banded flower fly eat aphids or that the most common gall on sweetbrier is called Robin's pincushion. Still, I am afraid I usually imitated Mole. If I didn't slide off a riverbank, at least I drifted from print to the soft edges of pages. What shone brightest from *An Almanac for Moderns* was not Donald Culross Peattie's ramble through a year, but an account penciled along the margin of three pages beginning on the sheet describing April 6 and ending on April 8. "In the morning," I read, "I worked in the greenhouse amid the varied colors and heady perfumes of carnations, poppies and calceolarias—taking daffodil bulbs from the earth that held them when they produced their beautiful yellow blooms—and putting them in crates for storage —until next Easter time when they will again come to life and gladden the hearts of people who are starved for beauty and color after a long, dark winter. In the afternoon I worked digging a ditch around the base of a foundation of a new house. I worked and smelled the earth, and I got it on my shoes and on my hands and legs."

University administrators forever preach the importance of research. Most research is simply messing about gone-uptown and gentrified. Still, I like to stick my oar in once or twice a year, just to show people that I am capable of rowing profound waters. To what Easter, I wondered, was the gardener referring when he wrote in the *Almanac?* Peattie's book was published in 1935, and the library's copy was part of the fourth impression, printed like the first edition in 1935. Because the fourth impression did not appear simultaneously with the first printing, I guessed that the gardener did not describe Easter, 1935. Still, since the handwriting was so faded, I reckoned the gardener must have written in the 1930s or '40s. "Most likely, Easter, 1936," I told Vicki. Research, of course, would reveal the truth, and the next day I hurried upstairs to the Information Desk. On the landing outside the first floor, a stranger delayed me. He told me he owned a black cat named Binky. Three weeks ago he came home late at night and found Binky lying dead on the road in front of his house. "Smushed by a tractor-trailer, all his 'gorpals' out," the man said. So that Caitlin, his daughter, would not see Binky in the morning and become upset, the man fetched a snow shovel from his garage and after scraping the cat off the pavement buried it in the backyard. "But guess what?" the man said. "When I opened the door the next day, Binky was curled up beside the *Hartford Courant.* Instead of Binky I buried Prune, my neighbor's pet. Isn't that just the cat's meow?" "You bet," I said. "That takes all dog."

At the Information Desk a librarian found a world almanac or booktionary, as Loppie Groat calls it, and I researched dates of Easter. In 1935, Easter was on April 21. The following year Easter fell on April 12. Since the gardener began his description of lifting bulbs on the page devoted to April 6, I didn't think it likely he read Peattie's book in either 1935 or 1936. In 1937 Easter occurred on March 28, over a week before the man began his account. In 1942 and again in 1953, however, Easter fell on April 5, and that evening I asked Vicki's help in interpreting the research and deciding in which of the two years the man wrote in the *Almanac.* "Neither," Vicki said. "Nobody pulls bulbs the day after Easter. Real gardeners let them bloom longer."

"They do?" I said. "Damn straight," Vicki said. "March 28 is the day. 1937 is the year. Any fool can see that. You must be suffering from Information on the Brain."

Fashioned from words and numbers, dates have long intrigued me, seeming coordinates on planes that appear to locate everything in time and space but which actually graph little. This fall I read a shelf of books written by William Hamilton Gibson, an artist and naturalist. Popular at the end of the nineteenth century, Gibson lived in Washington, Connecticut, and in April when the aromatic odorums of high educational talk blight spring, I may drive to Washington and saunter the byways Gibson described. This fall, though, I avoided such variables and concentrated on grids of dates. On December 24, 1897, the library of Storrs Agricultural College purchased a copy of Gibson's *My Studio Neighbors*. The book cost $1.67 and raised the holdings of the library to 5,434 books. A modest number of people met Gibson's studio neighbors as the book was borrowed only once in 1900, twice in 1902, then once again in 1903, 1907, 1908, 1913, 1919, and finally 1931. Gibson died in 1896. A biography appeared in 1902 and enjoyed a surge of popularity, being checked out six times in 1902. Interest ebbed quickly, though, and the book was not borrowed again until 1905. Ten years passed before another reader checked the book out in 1915. Before the next reader took out the book and the last library stamp appeared on the cover, thirteen additional years rolled past.

I did not spend the entire fall doing research in the library or dozing therapeutically above athletic fields. Reading influences messing about. In 1890 Gibson's *Strolls by Starlight and Sunshine* was published. After reading the book, I decided to wander Storrs, not by starlight, however, as no Ratty accompanied me and I didn't fancy slipping into the Fenton River some dark evening. Gibson entitled one of his books *Sharp Eyes*. Not just a lover but also a student of Nature, Gibson described relationships between things. In contrast, I saw only a miscellany of discrete objects. Still, objects are good enough. One morning four bluebirds perched on bittersweet in the backyard. That afternoon a fox trotted through the dell, and a red-tailed hawk hunched on an oak, looking like an urn shelved against the sky. Above the periwinkle a hornets' nest spun out of shape into shags. After Vicki hung bird feeders on the garage, the woods shed gray squirrels, and a circus of chickadees began performing, dangling upside down on suet then flipping themselves into the air and landing upright atop the platform under the kitchen window.

Starlings careened around Horsebarn Hill, the flock billowing and wavering, floating loosely through breezes like a jellyfish, a lion's mane skidding across currents, lines of birds momentarily stretching rubbery like tentacles before being jerked back into the flock. Amid brambles a catbird's nest resembled a cereal bowl. From the bottom of the nest oozed strips of cellophane while a serving of bittersweet berries floated above roots across the top of the nest. In woods, swatches of cedar moss resembled yellow vests, dandifying logs. Trains of cones swept out from white pines. White with dry, cracked resin, the scales looked painted. At dusk a young possum bustled along the shoulder of a broken road. In summer sunshine overflows hours. In late fall brightness seems limited. Not wanting to waste light, I wandered days. Near the Fenton River where light shimmered off laurel, I stood and let silver shake around me.

Despite my desire to absorb daylight, I also rambled rain, watching purple seep through the bark of red pine and worrying about a black racer hibernating under a sheet of plywood. A bulldozer pushed stone over the entrance to the snake's den, and the snake burrowed through a ball of grass beneath the plywood. On damp days I thought about the snake lying like a black bone, and several times I wove grass into the mound above him. On rainy afternoons sound bowled heavy across the ground instead of rising and splintering. On misty days I stood in the Ogushwitz meadow and listened to the afternoon freight, passing through town on the far side of Route 32. Not only did water press the sound of the train closer to the ground, but it absorbed it, turning it through the air in damp beads, so that the whistle echoed then rolled into gray silence. In contrast, the Fenton rushed lightly past like a streamliner. Catching on hemlocks, the water sounded like bags of air shaking against one another.

Much as Mole learned to swim and to row, so people who mess about learn to enjoy things, albeit they do not float downstream on their knowledge. Unlike Josh, I don't have contempt for history. Last week history freshened an evening. Three days earlier Francis finished a term paper that described the conflict between President Truman and General Douglas MacArthur during the Korean War. To write the paper, Francis borrowed seven books from the university library. Domestications being slightly less felicitous than usual, as Googoo Hooberry would put it, I decided to absent myself from the hearth and return the books to the library. By the Circulation Desk I met Wally. In his arms were eight books, the sources of his son's paper on Sacco and Vanzetti. "Things are cooking at home," he said. "I just thought I would bring the books back and mess around here for a while until the kitchen cools." "Good for you," I said, "there's nothing half so much worth doing."

In the Dark Wood

*L*ast month one of my essays appeared in a book entitled *In a Dark Wood: Personal Essays by Men on Middle Age*. The editor took the title from Dante. "In the middle of the journey of our life," Dante wrote, "I found myself in a dark wood where the straight way was lost." Middle-aged I am. Lost I'm not. Not only that but the woods which I roamed this November were not dark. Although rainy and cold, and sometimes snowy, the woods were open. Trees were bare, but my days, and nights, were not gloomy. In contrast to youth whose vision is obscured by leaves, I see clearly. Unlike youth I know straight paths don't exist. Instead of fretting time away battering through brier and branch, I saunter moments, my steps weaving arabesques that lead nowhere. Unable to see beyond the immediate, youth imagines a wood in which people live forever, in which success blooms just beyond the next patch of brambles. By middle age a walker knows that thickets of brambles clump one behind another like buttons down a cardigan sweater.

In a November wood, perspective expands, and the far draws close, be the far a century ahead or the close a past millennium. Instead of imagining future pleasure, I enjoy the moment. Rather than longing for pergolas unseasonable and soporific with grape, I notice lone asters, the petals scraggly and gap-toothed but the disks pink and warm. The university pool is fifty meters long. So that more people can swim at the same time, a walkway divides the pool into halves. Water flows under the walkway, and the walkway itself is so light that removing it before swim meets takes only minutes. Last Wednesday water in the pool was chilly. After swishing my right foot across the surface of the water, I turned to the woman standing next to me. "This half is really cold," I said. "I'm going to swim in the other end. The water there is warmer." The woman bent over and dangled her hand in the water. "Yipes," she said. "The water here is cold. I'll join you in the other half." An hour later as I left the gymnasium, the woman approached me. "Thank you for telling me about the warm end," she said. "I could not have swum in that cold water." "You're welcome," I said, hurrying off.

For the person whose vision is not clouded by youthful dream, November woods are rarely dark. From the pool I went to a lecture hall where I taught one hundred and thirty students. I arrived in the room fifteen minutes before class. Since students had not appeared, I prowled. Eight rows above the podium, a table and a chair sat on a landing. Unlike the tops of desks, which were so hard that students could not write upon them, the table was soft. Scratched across the table was a command that cheered me so much that I didn't dismiss class until six minutes after the bell rang. "End it!! END the torture!! Stop talking! Let us go!" a student demanded. "END CLASS NOW!"

Because leaves have fallen and I can see deep into the woods, not only do I expect less of others but I demand less of myself. The middle-aged person I now am is more relaxed than the youth I once was. Zeal does not undo me. Lecturing to the class after the period ended resembled something done by my friend Josh, not something I normally do. In fact I created Josh so that I would not be discommoded by ranting. Josh's hot flashes sear sensibilities, particularly those of young readers. When a reader harangues me about Josh's intemperance, I beg off, common-sensibly explaining that although I try to keep Josh sane "only a Bedlamite could hold me responsible for what an acquaintance says." Not surprisingly that explanation perturbs those who imagine straight ways and clip literature into geometric shapes, creating separate terraces for cones and spheres, fiction and nonfiction.

Not having to brush leaves aside as I saunter woods frees me to create sundry things, not just Josh. At times words themselves resemble leaves, and some days buds unfold luxuriantly. Unlike the leaves that blind youth, I control my words, spreading wax scale on a sentence; binding a four-lined plant bug to a verb; shaking mealybugs over one page, leaf miners on the next; and so arranging galls that they raise welts on paragraphs and irritate readers who want ideas and literature smooth and straightforward.

On Monday Hollis Hunnewell's "Arboretum Carnival" arrived in Carthage, Tennessee. Despite the name the carnival was a tented affair. Instead of evergreens clipped into odd shapes, the carnival exhibited human topiary. Just inside the tent The Preadamite Man lay on an ironing board. Tattooed on his chest was a checkerboard, and for a nickel two people could play a game. At birth, hosannas not howls rose spontaneously from the lips of The Little Flower Pot of Virtue, or The Born Miracle, as he was sometimes called. Not only had The Born Miracle memorized the book of Deuteronomy, but he was able to describe migrations of the Lost of Tribe of Israel, "from the desert sands to the clay hills of Middle Tennessee," as Hollis put it, "right smack-dab down to Main Street."

A flock of Carthaginians discovered they were lost descendants of the Tribe. For eight cents the Miracle's father offered each of "the chosen people" a testimonial signed by his son and himself, "an accredited apostle and Professor of Doxology." "Praise God," Turlow Gutheridge exclaimed after scrutinizing the Professor. "The Age of Miracles has arrived. In his first life the Professor was Ishmial Bushong, a curtailer of capillary substance in Wartrace. In just ten days he has gone from shaving people to shearing lambs."

A yellow sprinkler sprayed water over the Palace of Dew Drops. Above the door of the Palace rose a gable ornamented with bargeboards, the edges of which had been cut into crosses. Painted red and with a tin roof, the Palace resembled a Gothic doghouse. More lively than its architecture, however, were the Palace's royal inhabitants, three baby armadillos named John the Baptist, Yam, and Ostrich— John the Baptist and Yam being females, and Ostrich male. Beside the Palace a Somnambulist sat upright on a cot, reading the Tennessee State Constitution. Because the carnival was open only during the day, the Somnambulist never left the cot. At dark the man's behavior changed. "The difference between what ain't going on now and what happens then being as great as the difference between night and day," Hollis said.

At the foot of the cot stood a bamboo cage. In the cage sat a man covered with white blotches. According to a placard pasted on the bars, the man had escaped from a Hindu Lunatic Asylum by dusting himself with Panjandrum Powder. The powder made people invisible. If a person wore the powder too long, though, his skin turned white. Unfortunately two days passed before the escapee felt safe enough to wash the powder off. For a year afterward the man hid in a mangrove swamp, living on curry and chutney. "Not once during that year did he taste grits or fried chicken," the placard stated, "and it's a miracle he survived." Eventually the man was rescued by an Egyptian paddling a felucca and wearing "Nile green socks." Although the Egyptian never revealed his name, he presented his socks to the man. Hanging beneath the placard was a box with a glass front containing the socks. Reaching just above the ankle, the socks were short and had thin elastic tops, "size six," Turlow said, "the kind which keeps a body's feet from perspiring when he wears magic trotter cases."

Twice every afternoon Rosa Maybloom sang Christmas carols. The Two Little Sunbonnets accompanied her, the older playing a guitar, and the younger a fiddle. The apostle introduced Rosa, calling her a canorous wonder and urging crowds to become "ear witnesses." "Her warbling apparatus," he said, drawing upon his previous existence for metaphor, "will make your hair stand on both ends." After hearing Rosa sing, the mockingbird, Hollis testified, committed suicide. "Farewell berries and birdlets. Farewell treetops and telephone poles. I'm outsung," the bird cried before plunging into a horse trough.

Admission to the carnival being only five cents, Hollis increased takings by selling patent medicine. His Double Cornucopia and Balsamic Liver Pad, he said, "cured grip, heart wobble, the jumping toothache, and hydrophobia; eradicated bunions and corns; lowered the high fantods and loosened cramp of the eyebrows; turned green lips red; spun the tumblers of lockjaw; and when placed on the floor was rough on rats." "Yes," the apostle harmonized, "I seen it draw teeth from the mouth of a cannon and cure pain in the head of a nail." For folks whose Sunflower of Hope had gone to seed and who looked like the last of pea time on a pole, Hollis suggested a Caloric Glass Treatment, guaranteed to increase "nutrimental stamina." The glass was strapped to a wood box resembling a coffin. Once a sufferer stretched out in the box, Hollis closed the door and plugged in the glass. A blue light then bathed the patient with "aqua forty," or "aqua fifty," Turlow said, "for that somebody willing to pay six more cents." In addition to selling patent medicines and miracle cures, Hollis was agent for the Lightning Combination Sewing Machine and Vacuum Cleaner. "Made in Palestine-Jerusalem, New York, this device," he said, "is as virtuous as a sermon and as poetic as *House Beautiful.* It can knit, purl, stitch, hem, haw, cough, and chew tobacco. And when this cute little curly switch on the side is tweaked, it'll heel and point, lick dandruff off of butter, and fetch watches and country hams dropped down outhouse crappers."

"That stuff would curdle the Milky Way," Vicki said after I described the carnival. "Your brain must have donkeyfied." Eleven years my junior, Vicki still beats through bushes outside the dark wood. Not having aged beyond dream, she doesn't understand that nothing I write will increase, or decrease, sales of my books. Much as the open wood transforms past and future into the present, so it erases categories of relevant and irrelevant from the mind. What appears on a page is fitting, not because it heaves thought toward a goal, but simply because it follows. Before Vicki continued, I launched a poetic torpedo at her, calling her "my living sunbeam." Next I banged Josh into the conversation, changing the subject and blowing her criticism into farina. "Josh came by the office yesterday and asked me a riddle. Let's see if you can get it," I said. "What is the mother of a locomotive?" No straight way leading to the solution, Vicki was puzzled. "Bread," I answered. "A locomotive is an invention, and bread is a necessity, and as everybody knows, necessity is the mother of invention." Vicki left the room before I could tell her about the black-and-white photographs at the Masonic Temple in Carthage. Accustomed to elevating the ordinary into the mystical, seeing, for example, uprightness lurking within a crowbar and hearing the last trumpet in the ringing of a pickax, the brothers entitled the show "The Noncolorists Exhibition."

Josh is a Mason, an officer of his chapter, Grand Master of the Second Veil, to be exact. Josh knows that matters like the Caloric Glass interest me, and last month he revealed some of the tony greetings used at his lodge. When the High Priest enters the Temple, he says, "Syobolleh," an ancient Babylonian word roughly equivalent to the

English phrase "hello boys." For their part the King and the Scribe, sometimes joined by the Captain of the Host, answer, "olleh" or "odwoh." After squatting in the East, the High Priest looks around then asks "gnageht fotsereht serehw" which scholars have translated as "where's the rest of the gang?" At this point Josh becomes part of the ritual. He places his sword flat on the ground. Then after heisting up the skirts of his purple robe, he hops back and forth over the blade three times before speaking. Usually he says, "emstaeb." But on formal occasions when the Pot of Manna perches atop Gad on the Breastplate, he speaks solemnly, saying, "wonki fimnad."

Vicki is perturbed because my essays lack high purpose. "They don't facilitate, much less go anywhere," she said the other day. Things done for a purpose inevitably go wrong. Life is better, and usually longer, if a person takes things by the invisible handle and leaves shoveling and making mistakes to others. The Principal Sojourner of Josh's lodge scrutinized days as intensely as he studied The Tetragrammaton. He refused to act spontaneously and planned all his actions, even eating. "Always sit by windows in restaurants," he told Josh, "and you'll get large portions." Successful plans bring surprising results. The Sojourner's planning worked. Waiters inevitably served him heaping meals. Unfortunately he soon resembled a lard bucket, and one morning as he was sitting down to masticate a platter of cow heels, fried green tomatoes, and buttermilk pie, a cardiovascular belch spoiled breakfast and ruined his appetite forever. Actually culinary planning cracked the keystone of Josh's Royal Arch Chapter. As might be expected, the Treasurer was penurious, and to save money on food, he ate okra at every meal. Soon he saved so much money that he became wealthy and was able to afford an elegant, albeit unexpected, funeral.

Despite examples of intention's leading to the grave, I occasionally attempt to accommodate pages to the age and write with salubrious purpose. Blather about "catamitical hymeneal rites," as my friend Front Page says gals in the back rooms of the *New York Times* refer to same-sex marriages, has cluttered newspapers recently. The human male is a low creature, "a middling order of toad," according to Turlow Gutheridge. "If marrying an owl, a tumblebug, or even a woman will help a male lead a moral life, then bring on the parson," Josh said recently, suggesting, that "if an Episcopalian refuses to marry the dearly beloveds then a healer can be hired from one of the higher faiths, perhaps from the Chamber of Commerce." For once I agreed with Josh, and I decided to marry Mr. Billy Timmons to another man. The organist at the Tabernacle of Love, Mr. Billy was an old Carthaginian. His mother Big Mealy Timmons owned and ran the Butterburg Slaughterhouse and Dairy north of town. As Mr. Billy's hankerings for the hirsute were a little out of order, especially since his bride would not give birth four months after the wedding, so Big Mealy's matrimonial doings were also slightly irregular. "Big Mealy don't waste money buying second- and third-hand husbands," Loppie Groat said. "She just leases husbands and turns them in when their clutches start slipping and their carburetors begin to leak." "Folks at the Tabernacle of Love wouldn't object to Mr. Billy's marriage," I told Vicki. "He's the best musician in Smith County. There's not another organist in the state who can play 'Whispering Hope' and 'Trade My Name for a Piece of Tail' better than Mr. Billy. If Mr. Billy started attending the Baptist Church on Main Street, collections would drop off considerably at the Tabernacle." "Marrying off Mr. Billy is too with it," Vicki said, "and you are too deep in the wood to be up with anything, except maybe an animated catechism."

I followed Vicki's advice, and Mr. Billy remains an eligible man about town. Sometimes I regret the decision. If Mr. Billy had married, his mate would have been a new character. In part I create characters because the dark wood is silent. Instead of echoing the conversations of friends, the wood vibrates with memories. The longer I amble, however, the less I remember. Not only have most friends slipped from recollection but I have forgotten my own life. Two weeks ago I received my first electronic mail. The letter was hearty and intimate with particular memory. Alas, no matter how hard I whacked nearby trees, I could not make the wood vibrate with recollection, and my correspondent remains as mysterious as the operations of the Caloric Glass.

Vicki's two brothers celebrated Thanksgiving with us in Storrs. Along with families they brought a Jeroboam of Piper-Heidsieck champagne. Good bubbly affects me like the two biblical cities Seldom and Tomorrow influenced inhabitants. Not only does champagne provoke naughty behavior, but the only times I swig decent stuff are seldom and tomorrow, never often and rarely today. Soon after Vicki's brothers arrived, I was weaving the winding way. After lunch I stumbled against a thicket of saplings and jogged, if not memories, at least, what Josh calls, "the telephonic impulse." During the afternoon I called a score of friends and relatives in Virginia and Tennessee. Not until the last call, though, when I talked to my cousin in Richmond did the wood hum with particular memory. Recently my cousin's daughter got a divorce. While I talked to the girl, my cousin listened on an extension. Big Meally influenced the conversation. "The run of the spillway male is as nourishing as a vapor dinner and as appetizing as a bread poultice," I said, before suggesting the girl spend a few springs grazing wild asparagus before remarrying. "Great God!" my cousin exclaimed, slapping her receiver down. Suddenly memory bloomed, and I recalled why I had not heard from my cousin in a decade.

Although friendships wither in middle age, the dark wood remains vital. Across the ground, trailing arbutus twists evergreen. Among memories that fall and rumple over days like leaves, continuance sprouts quick. Last Sunday I rummaged through a stack of papers on the computer table. Amid the sheets I found sprigs of words, viny green paragraphs written by the children. "Loquisha's mane of medically grafted turquoise hair swept around her like a waterfall," Eliza began a story. "It hid her behind a curtain of shimmering blue and silver. Oblivious to the dreamlike image she presented, Loquisha brushed her hair back with one impatient, taloned finger. It didn't work. Sighing for what must have been the thousandth time that day, she gave up to the inevitable, and allowed her abnormally long wave of lustrous hair fly where it would. It was inconvenient, yes, but Loquisha had better things to do than worry over her hair."

Much as I left my account of cousinly doings incomplete, so Eliza did not finish the tale. In contrast, Edward completed "A Snowflake from Santa Clause," a story that transformed the dark wood into a forest of Christmas trees. The story took place in West Virginia on Christmas Eve. " 'Put your clothes on boys,' a woman said, barely turning from the cutting board," the first paragraph began. "There was silence for a moment, interrupted only by the dull whack of her knife. Up and down like clock-work, it went, slicing through tomato, pepper, and carrot without a second's pause or thought. In the background a fire crackled gently and flickered, throwing shadows across the wooden floor. On a bed beside the fire, the heavy, labored breathing of a sick man sleeping could be heard. The scene was almost too quiet, too peaceful to last for long. Like fate, a young boy's voice shattered the stillness of the log cabin. 'But why,' he whined, 'why must we shovel the entire driveway?' "

The boys' father was dying, and the family too poor to have the drive plowed. Outside the house, winter was magical. "The cool of night had set in," Edward wrote. "It filled every nook and cranny of the forest, covering the barren trees and leading sleepy-eyed creatures to their burrows. Above, a young moon shone brightly down. Its yellow light reflected off the snow-covered landscape and illuminated the forest. The trees stood naked, guarding the secrets and inner reaches of the mountains. Their vigil was silent. The forest was still, save for the occasional hoot of an owl and creaking of a tree as it bowed before some sudden gust."

While the boys shoveled, they talked, first wondering why their mother cried so often and then questioning the existence of Santa Claus. Suddenly a huge stag stepped from the shadows and stared at the boys, so entrancing them that they followed the animal into the forest. The deer was Prancer, and he led them to Santa Claus's sleigh. Santa's eyes not being as strong as they once were, he had steered too low and, brushing the tops of trees, had crashed into the forest. The sleigh toppled over, and Santa was pinned beneath a mound of presents. "His cheeks shone bright red," Edward wrote, "and a great long beard trailed away from his head, seeming to weave itself through the entire pile of presents." The boys freed Santa and stacked the presents back atop "the great red sleigh." Before galloping off into the sky, Santa took a small box from his coat and, giving it to the boys, told them not to open it until they were home. Once inside their cabin, John, the older boy, opened the lid of the box "and peered in. He gasped with wonder for before him was a magnificent perfect little snowflake. It lay on a purple cushion and sparkled as the light danced over it. Suddenly it lifted into the air as if an invisible string were pulling it. It twirled around and around and then disappeared. The boys were still gazing up in wonder when the hands of their father came to rest upon their shoulders." The magic snowflake brought the boys the best possible present, their father's health. On hearing her husband speak, the mother looked up from across the room, "joy and amazement written over her face. As the family gathered around the fire, the sounds of jingling and a great merry laugh drifted down the chimney." "Gee whiz," I said, sitting back in my chair, letting Edward's story slip out of my hand and slide onto my lap. "Gee whiz."

In the dark wood Christmas glitters even when bulbs don't shine. Until last Saturday the December sky resembled a cookie tray, flat and gray but occasionally silver at sunset when light scratched across the horizon like steel wool. On Saturday night the sky humped into a bowl then flipped over, dumping snow across Mansfield. Heavy and wet, the snow resembled suet pudding, curdling across the ground in meaty white lumps. At 7:53 Saturday night the lights went out. Power would not be switched on again until after dusk on Tuesday, one minute and seventy hours later. At nine o'clock I wandered into the small wood behind our house. Instead of dark the wood was luminous, sleeves of snow turning thin, palsied limbs into massive forearms and thighs. As I walked, fists of snow pounded the ground. Noise splintered around me. Snow bent then stripped branches from trees. When small limbs broke, the sound resembled thick cardboard being shredded or the slats of wooden fruit boxes forced double over wire bindings. Often snow broke a big tree like a maul a log. For a moment, shaking sprayed through the air, then the ground arched upward before collapsing into a muffled hummock.

For a long time I stood behind shortstop on the high school baseball field. Beyond foul lines trees pushed upward in a white glaze. Because their tops were invisible, trees seemed to curve over the field in fingers, forming a loose strainer, snow oozing through gaps like custard. Behind me power at the university banged off and on. Each time the electricity shut down, green exploded through the night, turning the sky above the field moldy. "When the power went off," Francis said later, "I seemed to be standing in the middle of an emerald."

On my return from the wood Vicki and the children met me in the front yard. "Trees are falling everywhere," Eliza said. "Let's walk around the circle." The walk frightened me. Wires danced up and down, and broken branches swayed over the road, pushing snow aside like brooms. Twice wires snapped like necklaces, and yellow sparks spilled over the snow. The next morning the sight was not so dreamy. Wires dangled over the road, resembling innards ripped from the belly of some vast machine. For the next two and a half days little was romantic, particularly for Vicki who hankers for straight ways. Vicki worried about losing food in the icebox. "I knew I should have bought a Double Cornucopia and Balsamic Liver Pad," I said Monday. "Hollis called it a first-class microbe destroyer. A smidgen prevents food from spoiling." In October I purchased a new icebox, and when the electricity returned on Tuesday, only a few things had gone bad. Milk soured, and ice cream in two half-gallon containers fell into the corners of the boxes, slumping out of texture and bulk like flesh on the hips of old men. Even so, Francis lapped up the remnants, quoting Loppie Groat, saying, "it may not be as refreshing as Hermon's dew, but it will do."

I don't own a wood stove, and the temperature fell to forty-four inside the house. On Monday afternoon when Vicki was away, I built a fire in the living room. I had not used the fireplace for six years because I worried that the chimney would catch on fire and late some night wake from a long smolder and burn the house down. The fireplace does not throw heat much beyond the hearth. Inside the fireplace, however, sits an insert with a blower attached to it. The blower pushes waves of heat into the room. Once the fire blazed, I plugged the blower into a wall socket, saying to myself, "Won't this surprise Vicki." Alas, I forgot the electricity was off. By the time Vicki came home, the fire had shrunk to ash.

We ate dinner at the kitchen table, take-out from a Chinese restaurant on Sunday and Domino's pizza on Monday. The table resembled an altar. Five candles flickered in the middle. Around them six flashlights stood on end, their beams throwing yellow saucers on the ceiling. We ate in gloves, stocking caps, and winter coats. For Chinese food the attire was suitable. Gloves, however, don't complement pizza, and throughout the meal I peeled mushrooms and pepperoni off the index finger of the glove on my right hand.

Evening conversation focused on electricity. On Monday afternoon at two o'clock, houses on the two streets that run into Hillside Circle and half the Circle itself got power back. The nine houses on the west side of the Circle remained black. "Why us?" Vicki moaned at dinner Monday night. Habit is an iron shirt. Carthage immediately popped into mind and out of mouth. "Why us? Why thus? Wharfo?" I said, wondering who among my fictional characters might say such a thing.

My wit did not warm Vicki. To melt her I launched another poetic torpedo, saying her "lips were red as a stove." The torpedo passed ignored through the talk. Beyond Vicki, however, my remark seemed to hit an iceberg as the atmosphere in the kitchen suddenly became chillier. Next I tried to jolly things up by describing the gastronomic plight of a cannibal marooned on a desert island with a skeleton. Vicki did not let me finish the story, and for the rest of the evening she remained frosty. Of course a bonfire of laughter would not have warmed the bedroom. Wearing three pairs of socks, a nightgown, two sweat shirts, and a stocking cap, Vicki became a mound builder and turned herself into an anthropological study. Men differ from women. I did not sleep in a cap or sweat shirt. On Sunday night I wore a pair of socks but kicked them off at one-thirty when my toes began to perspire. Because she felt as if she were "being cremated by cold," Vicki left the house early on Monday and Tuesday and spent both days at malls. Since classes at the university had ended, I stayed at home. Two or three times each morning I telephoned Northeast Utilities in hopes of learning when power would be restored.

"My behind has frozen and started cracking," I told a woman Tuesday. "In fact a big split has begun to run down the middle. You've got to turn the heat on." "I wish I could flip a switch for you, but I can't," the woman responded. "But if I were you, I'd haul ass right over to the drugstore and buy a pot of Vaseline." By Tuesday afternoon I was cold, and I went to a dentist's office an hour before an appointment just to sit in a warm room. As soon as the children came home from school, I sent them to the university library to do homework. Late Tuesday before the power came back on, I escorted Eliza to the gymnasium, where she showered. Eliza had not bathed since Wednesday, not that she minded. At eleven she is not bothered by grit. Neither is Edward, despite the clean narrative line of his Christmas story, and by the end of the blackout, he smelled like someone who spent evenings repairing the transmissions of sleighs. In contrast, cold does not bother Francis. Francis walks to school, and despite having to trudge through icy days, has worn shorts every day since September. On Sunday and Monday nights Francis showered at home, telling me the water was "almost warm."

Four streets in Storrs, including Hillside Circle, have university water and sewerage. Although electricity dried up, water ran, and we did not spray niter over a back fence. The houses on all the other streets in town rely upon electricity to pump water into sinks and toilets. "Discovering whose electricity was off was easy," Josh told me Monday. "Lines formed early at the stalls in the gymnasium. All I had to do was take roll." Even on hot days Josh can be sharper than an icicle. Particularly irritating to him are people who pass words off as deeds. "Brotherly love is free, but bread costs money," I once heard him say to a social engineer. "Now I understand the problems of homeless people who spend winters sleeping in boxes under bridges," a "career counselor" remarked to him on Tuesday. "No," Josh replied, "you only understand inconvenience. You are warm now. In a week the cold will be the stuff of disposable tea table conversation."

Vicki doesn't like Josh. After I described Josh's conversation with the counselor, she said, "I wish you would abandon him in that dark wood you've talked about so much recently." "All right," I agreed. "But I don't want him to spend December by himself. I will give him a brindle cat for a companion and serve them a large eel pie for dinner. Josh has a sweet tooth, and one of the 'emulgators' for sale at the carnival could provide dessert. Hollis called the cows 'mobile soda fountains whose lacteal faucets squirt ice cream instead of milk.'"

A New Dream

*W*henever Eliza runs a fever or piles too many blankets atop herself on the bed, she has night terrors. She dashes through the house and screams, "Don't kill me." To calm her I urge her to go to the lavatory. Afterward I give her a cup of cool water and bath her face. Sometimes we count aloud together. The terrors don't fade quickly. Monsters chase her from room to room. Afraid she will fall downstairs or jump from a window, I hold her tightly. She struggles to escape, but I don't let her go, the terror of what could happen to my little girl more frightening than any of the invisible creatures that stalk the night. Last week while holding her, I said, "sweetheart, you are just having a bad dream." Thrusting her hands in front of her face, almost as if my words were demons, she immediately shouted, "Somebody get me another dream!" "Please," she begged, staring at but not recognizing me, "please get me a new dream."

Would that I could have given my daughter a new dream. Alas, like curtains stripped from windows in a living room, age tears illusion from life. Instead of imagining blue spring rain tapping at window panes, I now see disappointment and cold, aching grief. When the children were babies, I wrapped my arms about them, and squeezing them imagined protecting them from hurt. I know better now. As I clutched Eliza, the sense of my own weakness welled within me and I regretted life itself. "It would have been better not to have been born," I thought, "than to have aged beyond dream."

In such darkness may lie the origins of religion and the transcendent "Let there be light." "Jesus," Slubey Garts once said, "paints the world white with his blood." Unlike Slubey I live in the afterglow of faith, that sentimental time just after sunset when clouds glow so richly that one almost believes day is dawning. Still, as stars shine yellow through the night, so bits of things prick dreamless days, providing, if not compensation for the absence of light, at least moments of delight. Just before Christmas Vicki and I ate lunch at The Tearoom. Before she opened The Tearoom, Sandy raised a family and worked in a greenhouse. "I didn't see many people," she said. "When I started The Tearoom, I was surprised to see how many different kinds there were." "A kid in my high school put a girl's contact lenses in his eyes," Mary said at the Cup of Sun. "What happened?" Vicki asked. "I don't know," Mary said. "They just took him away."

After Christmas Vicki and I and the children visited Princeton. One night after dinner Vicki's mother asked me to remove some pecans from the kitchen icebox. "They have been in the refrigerator for some time and are probably spoiled," she said. In the back of the freezing compartment I found nine packets of "Fresh Shelled Pecans." Each packet contained a pound of nuts. Taped around the packets were white papers. Written on the papers were the dates Vicki's mother put the nuts in the icebox. In November, 1978, she stored three pounds in the icebox; in December, 1982, two pounds; in November, 1983, two more pounds; and lastly in December, 1983, two pounds.

Things pile up in Princeton. One morning Vicki's mother decided to open her presents. The first present she opened was a calendar. Vicki's mother keeps five cats, and since a picture of a cat appeared above the days of each month, the calendar was almost a success. Unfortunately the calendar was for the year 1995, not 1997. Instead of opening the calendar when she received it in December, 1994, Vicki's mother dropped it atop a pile of boxes in the television room where it lay forgotten, much like the nuts in the kitchen.

Almost invariably, things that delight me are small. On New Year's Eve I walked across the university campus in Storrs. Near the bookstore I met an older woman singing, "The White Cliffs of Dover." "Just you wait and see," she said. "There'll be bluebirds over the white cliffs of Dover." That morning three bluebirds foraged through bittersweet in the back yard. "And the meadow will bloom again," I said, adding, "Happy New Year." "Happy New Year," she said, and the snow sparkled with diamonds.

Greed determines many dreams. According to a Basque story, an angel gave a poor man a hen that laid precious eggs. The hen laid one egg a day. When the man cracked the egg open, the white turned into silver and both the yellow and the shell became gold. For a while the man was happy. But wealth inevitably changed him. He became covetous, and instead of living contentedly on his farm outside Santiago de Compostela, he dreamed of owning a mansion in Madrid. No longer did the single egg satisfy him. Eventually he lost his reason, and one morning he chopped the chicken's head off and ripped open her body in order to get the hoard of eggs which he thought lurked inside. Greed produces more fools than genes, Turlow Gutheridge told the luncheon crowd at Ankerrow's Café, describing the time Hink Ruunt bought an ostrich in hopes of hatching pumpkins. "As usual Hink wanted too much," Turlow said. "Only one of the pumpkins hatched. He would have done better if he'd set the ostrich over a crop of cantaloupes."

Happiness sues wealth for divorce almost as much as it does poverty. "So far as I can see," Josh said yesterday, "sudden wealth plucks feathers from bluebirds and binds dreams to a low nest furnished with long cars and golden chamber pots." On the drive to Princeton I stopped at a McDonald's near Upper Montclair on the Garden State Parkway. Inside the door of the restaurant stood a rack of flyers advertising Atlantic City, "America's Favorite Playground." For twenty-five dollars four people could spend a night in the Luxury Inn, the Budget Lodge, or the Absecon Motor Lodge, "only 8 minutes from Atlantic City." "Nobody Entertains Like Us," declared a folder published by the City Convention and Visitors Authority.

Outside the Budget Lodge a sign towered over boxwood. Under the name of the motel the word VACANCY stood out in flashing red letters. Beneath it a broad billboard proclaimed "Free Coffee • HBO • Day Rates • Fax • Jacuzzi • Never Undersold." "The stuff of dreams," Francis said, looking at the flyers. "Yes," I said. "Never follow another man's luck, particularly to blackjack and roulette." "Forbidden," Turlow Gutheridge said, "is the wise man's motto." I've never been in a casino or associated with people who gambled. "If you pat the cat who plays with snakes," Slubey Garts warned his congregation last Sunday, "poison will seep through your fingers and work its way to your heart." "Atlantic City offers," the Convention Authority stated, "12 action-packed casinos for 24-hour gaming excitement." Age makes a person wary not simply of taking chances but of excitement itself. On New Year's Eve Vicki, the children, and I ate popcorn and on the VCR watched *James and the Giant Peach,* a movie adapted from Roald Dahl's children's book. In the movie little Henry Trotter flew from Britain to New York inside a huge peach. Accompanying Henry were a wonderful lot of New Year's companions: Glow-worm, Centipede, Spider, Earthworm, Lady Bug, and Old-Green-Grasshopper.

During the Christmas holiday Vicki and I accepted only one invitation. Just before we left the house, Eliza slammed the door to the upstairs bathroom. Forty-five years old, the lock on the door broke, sealing off Eliza and the only bathtub in the house. For fifty minutes I struggled to unlock the door, removing every screw and all the moving parts I saw. Eventually I telephoned Mr. Arsenault, the locksmith. He arrived an hour later. An hour and a half after he appeared and long after dessert had been served and eaten at the dinner party, he was still working on the door. Eventually, he removed molding from the wall and released the door and Eliza. I ordered pizza from Paul's, and we ate dinner at the kitchen table. "A night to remember," Vicki said. I pulled a brochure from Atlantic City out of a pile on the table. "No matter what you do for fun," I said, emending the flyer, "home's the place to play. Excitement, attractions, activities. Whether it's just the two of you, the whole family, or the whole company, you'll never run out of things to do."

Next to money, people covet long life more than anything else. Dreams of immortality spread epidemic through the early middle years, ages forty to fifty-five. Beyond fifty-five, long life becomes the monster of night terrors. Instead of drooling through decades, one dreams of clean, swift endings: the slamming of a door or a book's being banged shut. In their forties, however, dreamers often subject themselves to regimens of diet and thought in hopes of prolonging life. Last month in Red Boiling Springs, Sister Abraham, a faith doctor, sold a dozen beehives. "Much as his familiars, buzzards and tumblebugs, hate sweetness, so Death feeds upon the rotten and the bitter," the Sister declared. "Eat honey every day, and you'll grow so sweet Death will let you sit on the porch and shuck corn and shell beans until the cows come home."

Of course some people clutch life even while the wheels of the undertaker's cart rattle up the drive. In Carthage walking corpses visited Daughter Ruth or Madame Cora. Ruth practiced ceromancy. Using a silver spoon with a thin handle and a minute bowl, she scooped wax out of patients' ears. After stirring the wax into a mug of green tea, she gave the blend to the patient to drink, saying "nothing cures a graveyard cough faster." Afterward she read the tea leaves, always predicting that her customer would recover and enjoy a prosperous and astonishingly long life. For her part Cora practiced cephlomancy and burned the heads of cats. Turlow Gutheridge claimed that the rats in Carthage paid her a retainer. Be that as it may, however, once a skull was roasted, Cora broke it open with a silver ball peen hammer and spread the brains of the cat over a silk handkerchief. Next she poured goat's milk over the brains, the milk, she told one hopeless case, coming from a flying nanny. Lastly Cora read the brains, hope always steaming upward from the porridge of feline and ruminant.

According to Turlow, only the number of the sick limited the ingenuity of the medical fraternity. In the Belle Meade section of Nashville, Brother Dave made a fortune out of gastromancy, the study of ventral flatuliloquence. Unlike most faith doctors, Dave was educated. He attended the Juilliard School of Music in New York, and when not on call, played percussion in the Nashville Symphony. Dave's trained ear determined his prognosticatory response, Turlow explained, the diagnosis depending upon the tempo of patients' emissions, whether they were *largo, allegro scherzando, maestoso, poco a poco,* or *andantino cantabile.* After buying a bad ham from Hink Ruunt, Loppie Groat suffered *con fuoco prestissimo.* Shortly after eating the ham, Loppie went to Nashville to purchase a jenny as a companion for Jeddry, his mule. In hopes of restoring his inner doings to a normal *adagio,* Loppie visited Belle Meade. "I searched for Brother Dave everywhere," Loppie recounted, "at Green Hills Grocery, at a meeting of Alcoholics Anonymous at St. George's Church, and on the back nine at the Belle Meade Country Club. Nobody ever heard of Brother Dave, and I wouldn't be surprised if that damn old Turlow didn't make him up out of thin air."

In December, dreams swirl through days like snow. Children imagine sleighs sagging with presents. Robbie, the young son of my friend Bruce, made a list of toys he wanted for Christmas. The list was long, and Robbie realized some of the items were expensive. "Daddy," he said, "I know you can't buy me all these things. You and Mommy can just give me a Nerf ball. My friend Billy got most of these toys last year, and Billy is not a very good boy. I'm better than Billy, and I've tried hard to be good this year. Santa Claus is fair, and he will give me what I ask for." Dreams are hard masters, particularly the dreams of children. Robbie received most of the toys on his list, and if the truth be known, Bruce received a wonderful present, too: his son's innocent words. When I heard the story, bluebirds soared over the white cliffs. The shepherd tended his sheep, as the song put it, and the rank pasture of adult life became a meadow blooming again, sweet and soft with flowers.

Many of the cards Vicki and I received this Christmas depicted, if not that meadow, at least an edenic world. Across the fronts of cards animals wandered, not simply protected but treasured. Often wrapped in snow, the animals resembled ornaments for trees, decorations hung through generations, stored in the attic amid tissue paper and brought out once a year, triggering memories of family, both of immediate family and of that mythological family who wandered the first garden, animals and man companions, all saying "Merry Christmas to all, and to all a good-night." On a card a rabbit crouched in a warm bed under the boughs of a white pine, a December cultivar with red berries rolling along green needles. Three chickadees perched above the rabbit chattering like kindling snapping on a hearth. On another card a stag and doe stood side by side in a forest, silver moonlight washing over them protectively. Bears appeared on several cards: teddy bears sitting before a fireplace eating chocolate-chip cookies, polar bears sunning on an ice flow, then a brown bear beside a panda, both animals staring at a white dove falling from the sky like an arrow.

Dogs appeared on several cards, all inhabitants of the peaceable kingdom, none snarling or growling. A dachshund stood on its hind legs, holding a sprig of holly in its mouth. Six minute white reindeer pulled Santa Claus and his sleigh over the head and down the muzzle of a weimaraner. Santa Claus likes dogs. Beneath a Christmas tree he set a brown and white puppy with a red ribbon tied around its neck.

Earlier in the day he knelt beside a duck pond and patted a young golden retriever. The puppy was one of four litter mates. One of his siblings chewed a green ribbon while the other two sniffed a duck decoy. Dogs often appeared on photographs accompanying cards. While Missy, Lucy, and Ramsey—a spaniel, a shepherd, and a corgie—stretched out in a golf cart on one card, on another an English setter sat on a rock between two blond girls, bouquets of daisies white and yellow behind them. In truth George and Penny appeared on our card, Edward holding George, and Eliza, Penny. "We wouldn't be a family without the dogs," Edward said. Children always appeared on cards composed of photographs, youth being a frail vessel but one sturdy enough in a December dreamtime to embody the unspoken hopes of adults. A six-year-old boy stood on the front steps of his house, smiling and wearing a double-breasted blue suit. A baby girl wrapped her arm around her father's neck while a four-year-old wearing a blue velvet dress with a lace collar sat in her grandmother's lap, the grandmother's lumpy hands resting lightly on the child's small fingers. Scenes from past times appeared on many cards. Smoke rose in bonbons from farmhouse chimneys. A dappled horse pulled a sleigh down a country lane. In an Edwardian townhouse a mother stood on a ladder and lit candles on a tree. At the foot of the ladder a boy in page-boy dress blew a tin horn and galloped into Christmas on a wooden rocking horse.

Letters accompanied a file of cards. Only parents with grown children sent letters. Unlike the pictures of small children before whom the future stretched hazy and golden, the letters described achievement and turned vague imaginings into lawyers and artists, people who had hardened out of possibility into identity. How sad, I thought, that fifteen years could transform a butterball with blond hair into a stockbroker in San Francisco. Grown children not only conformed to but exploited the world. Only on cards do people seem to dream of the peaceable kingdom. Even so the photograph on one card brought that dream into clear, destructive focus. A nineteen-year-old boy knelt in snow, holding up the head of an elk he had shot. "Why would anybody put such a picture on a Christmas card?" Vicki asked. "Well," I said, stumbling over words; "the parents are from the south, and this is the first big animal the boy has shot. He's been bloodied and has grown up." "That's just something you read in a book," Vicki said. "Our children are young, and I don't want them to grow into such a picture. I don't want them to see this card." "I agree," I said, dropping the card into the waste can, knowing that someday the peaceable kingdom would slip from dream and our babies would also be bloodied.

Spontaneous with joy, one or two letters seemed in tune with the season. "Our two little girls," Ron wrote from Canada, "are still a few years from the time when boys will start to interfere with sanity—so we enjoy life day by day. This year's big treat will be a week in Disney World right after Christmas." From Texas Don wrote that his daughter Abigail had been accepted at Sewanee, his old college, adding that he had been elected a trustee. "So the happy cycle will begin again. You are a good guy, and I love you. Merry Christmas." A few letters contained oddities. A friend who left Connecticut four years ago wrote from California that he was a single course short of becoming "a Transpersonal Psychologist." "What's a transpersonal psychologist?" Eliza asked. "You don't want to know," I said. "But if some fellow introduces himself as one, grab your brain and run." Taped inside one card was a small piece of paper, measuring three by four inches. At the bottom of the paper an acquaintance jotted a note. Stamped across the top of the paper was "New once-daily Arimidex anastrozole 1 mg tablets," the Arimidex printed in red, all the rest in black.

Fiction distracts me from dreams. Instead of imagining rich futures for the children, I fashion the low doings of characters in Carthage, Tennessee, the hard particulars of nouns and verbs, pinning me to, if not the actual, at least the concrete. In December members of the Church of the Chastening Rod criticized Slubey Garts's use of flowers. A quarrel blossomed, and the praying brothers in the Amen Corner of one church were soon tossing bouquets of thorny words at the agonizing sisters in the Hallelujah Corner of the other church. A thriving minister and entrepreneur, Slubey raised his sermons around common-sensible statements such as "there are no fans in hell" and "the fat cow is tied by its teeth."

Consistency exists only in dreams. Although Slubey's sermons were plain, he enjoyed flowers, and the Tabernacle of Love was always colorful with blooms. Spring, he once said, was a "fallen rainbow that lifted thoughts beyond clouds." In September he placed pitchers of goldenrod in the windows of the Tabernacle, calling goldenrod "the Christian flower," the bunches of blossoms "congregations blooming in God's pure sunshine"—unlike, he said, "sinners blowing beneath hot lights in the Midnight Inn in Lebanon." Slubey planted willows and boxwood in the Pillow of Heaven Cemetery and encouraged parishioners to send flowers to funerals. "I'd rather swallow mist for lunch and listen to stories as fresh as last winter's snow," he said, "than to plant a soul under a bare bed." In sermons Slubey mentioned flowers, calling the morning glory Christ's nightcap, and dodder His shoelaces. If young women studied the prickly fruits of sweet gum, they would remain chaste, no matter the temptation "to put up coal or plant taters." Slubey went too far, at least for the Church of the Chastening Rod, when he said that Michael did not carry a sword when he drove Adam and Eve from Eden but a gladiola, its orange blossoms flaming. The word *gladius*, Slubey explained, meant sword in Latin, an explanation that Malachi Ramus labeled gibble-gabble.

For the Church of the Chastening Rod, Slubey's fondness for flowers smacked of Rome and addictions to candlesticks and watering cans. "The time is drawing near," Carsten Slipperback said, referring to Purgatory, "when Slubey will accuse good Christians in heaven of not bowing to the Fifth Moon or of forgetting to sprinkle themselves with Hog Hoof Powder. He will turn the sanctified into convicts and stripping the white robes of glory from their backs force them into striped pajamas." Not only was Slubey called "a tumbler of coins" and a "living mortification," but he was "a base horticulturist, guilty of herborising."

The chapel of the Church of the Chastening Rod was austere. A pulpit shaped like a coffin stood on the stage. At the back of the stage an American flag mildewed on a pole. On the wall above the flag was a picture of Jesus, his mouth as straight as an irrigation ditch and his hair and eyes black as bottomland. Having banished both the cross and flowers from the building, condemning them as remnants of paganism, Malachi Ramus thought Slubey's appreciation of flowers idolatry and called his fondness for goldenrod "hankerings after the golden calf." When a member of the Church died, people did not send flowers to the graveyard. Instead the family of the dead person presented mittens and occasionally scarves to mourners. Carsten Slipperback's wife Ornatta knitted the tokens, decorating them with winged death's heads. One evening after Malachi attacked flowers, saying that harlots flocked nightly about their blossoms, Pump Muddle chopped down two horse chestnuts growing beside town hall. "Horse chestnuts," Pump told Sheriff Baugham later, "are the devil's own unnatural tree. Instead of porcupine eggs, they lay flowers and teach people to sleep their lives away by the side of the road instead of drinking the blood of Lamb and struggling uphill to Canaan."

For the most part Slubey remained above the fray and let his deacons skirmish with the Church of the Chastening Rod. The Sunday after Pump Muddle sawed down the horse chestnuts, however, Slubey urged his congregation to avoid "ravenous frugality that reduced God's gifts to switches and ashes." "When grasshoppers call on fields," he said, "farmers will weep." Unlike Slubey, who obliquely mined a cavern under the Church of the Chastening Rod, Proverbs Goforth charged the front stoop, calling the congregation blind mouths, volecatchers, black fleas, pickled tumors, and tin alligators dancing on the altar of lunacy. "Because he was born eleven and a half months after the death of his father, Malachi Ramus," Piety Goforth declared, "has always been as proud as a half-wit with two peckers." Piety called Carsten Slipperback "the Emperor of Mustard Land" and said he had a liver as big as a shovel and "a mouth like a wheelbarrow, always full of second-hand meat." After listening to Piety's harangue, I decided that words had run more to blight than to fruit and so I stopped describing the quarrel. Once I quit writing, the churches also dropped the quarrel. Having been singed by the heat of controversy, both churches decided to follow the advice of the old adage, "Don't use poison when you can kill with honey." While Slubey brought Pharaoh Parkus to town for a revival and prayed for "all his brothers and sisters in Christ, no matter how misguided," Malachi declared that "His transparent hand" had pointed out the error of his ways. One Lord's Day he led his congregation to Town Hall and planted two magnolias beside the building, both trees *magnolia grandiflora.*

The winters depicted on Christmas cards resembled hearths. Farmhouses glowed in the centers of cards like logs, snow piled around them in ashy mounds. About the edges of cards forests hung like andirons brassy and colorful with decorations: holly, its berries bigger than lollipops; bluebirds and cardinals clipped onto twigs; an orchard of fruits, apples, pears, oranges, and limes; and then a manger of animals resembling windup toys, rabbits, horses, deer, and a lone skunk, the good cheer of season so warming him that he broke hibernation.

Instead of pulling place snugly about one like blanket, actual winter opens the landscape. Woods resemble clean pages, and vision tumbles quickly over margins. December, though, is family month. Instead of wandering off the notebook and dreaming beyond the page, I wrote the immediate across days, my penmanship flowing across mantle and window sill, covering them with boughs of pine, Christmas knickknacks looping and swirling through the needles. Outdoors I confined myself to the lines between trees, filling them with jottings. Late in afternoons Canada geese gleaned Bean Hill looking like smudge pots. Overhead the wind buffeted a ring-billed gull, knocking him down the air toward the old dairy barn. In the woods grapevines cinched themselves through trees in cables. Paths froze rougher than tongues. I studied the big ashes above the ski slope. The trees twisted more willfully than the speech of anyone in Carthage. A massive limb reached out emphatically then suddenly shattered into stutters of tentative branches. While one limb flowed upward toward lyricism, another sagged down, lichens pocking it. Here a limb staggered like the palsied sentences of old age. There a branch swung youthful and naive. The strength of one branch frittered into twigs. Another leaned over the hill, ponderous and solemnly stupid.

Down the slope deer chewed the trunks of cherry trees. Pasted around twigs were the shiny cases of tent caterpillars, resembling rounds of ribbon candy. Inside cases eggs clustered like minute pickle jars stored on shelves too small to hold them, dabs of turquoise sealing the jars to each other so they would not fall and shatter. Green spleenwort crept through roots above the spring while leafy liverwort dozed atop moss. A rotten stick stuck out of the ground, *hydnochaete olivacea* feathery around it, making decay flutter orange at the edge of sight. Amid rocks around the spring the stems of maidenhair fern shined like cordovan while the leaves scrolled inward out of existence. In the marsh, seed capsules wound upward in necklaces about stalks of sensitive fern. Strings tying the capsules had frayed, and the purple beads had begun to split and exhale spores. In the sunshine the calyxes of mad-dog skullcap gleamed, those still containing fruit humped, their tops pinched into minute caps. The calyxes from which nutlets had spilled lost their caps and resembled shovels.

I walked through the woods toward the beaver pond. The night before, a great horned owl had caught a rabbit. On a log sprawled the rabbit's right foot, lower and upper leg, and part of the animal's spine, the ribs flaring like fans and the leg bones joined at right angles, jutting like steps. The foot was four inches long from the tip of the nails to the heel. The owl ripped most of the meat from the rabbit, but tight ligaments still bound red hunks to bones. Near the Fenton River a robin's nest was plastered to an elderberry, the deep dish abandoned to mud and grass after a spring and summer of baking.

Virgin's bower curled smoky through swamp dogwood in the Ogushwitz meadow. Chickadees pattered gaily through scrub while from the far side of the river came the thin call of a sparrow. Sprays of berries clung to privet, splattering the bush blue like delft. Dodder broke from nannyberry and slipped to the ground in stiff bundles. Hemlocks insulated the riverbank, the needles holding warmth like down. In November a storm wrenched trees from the bank and dropped them into the water. From the limbs of fallen trees racks of long-necked jugs of ice dangled over the river. On Christmas Eve I walked beside the river until dusk. Gray clouds pushed swollen over a ridge, turning the dark blue sky brown. Wisps of light cloud slipped from the gray and drifted like loose ice sugary through a cold stream. The next morning the sun shone like silver. Barbara and Geoff, Eliza's aunt and uncle, sent her a chain and a heart-shaped locket from Tiffany's. After putting the locket on, Eliza looked in the mirror and said, "Christmas is a dream." I glanced out the kitchen window. A downy woodpecker clung to suet. A squirrel sat on a limb flicking its tail like a dishrag. A blue jay flew into the lilac, and four snowbirds huddled in the bittersweet. I had not seen bluebirds since the beginning of the month. But I knew they would return in spring. All I had to do was wait and see.

Naughty French Dancing Girls

"*D*ancing girls?" Vicki said when I mentioned the title. "I suppose that means another essay about bugs." "Yes," I said. The answer wasn't truthful. I am a sunny-day insect fancier. Finding bugs in January takes work. Ice seals logs to the ground, and cold freezes loose bark to tree trunks. Moreover, I have never met any lively French girls, much less naughty ones, ready at a beat's notice to drop dainty propriety and spinning free from the social minuet strut exuberant into the cancan. I chose the title because I liked the way the words sounded, and, in part, I suppose, because occasionally I imagine doing a bit of high-stepping. Although hankering has never bounced me out of my swivel chair, sometimes I trip over the doings of that most warm-hearted of all dancers, Venus.

According to an old Boeotian tale, Earth was once dry. One favorable spring elongation Venus lured Earth from his orbit. While promenading with Venus, Earth's sedate waltz around the sun became a fox trot, then a jig and finally a zodiacal pasadouble. Unaccustomed to anything faster than a do-si-do, Earth overheated. Instead of fire, water exploded from his volcanoes, creating the oceans, the salt in the seas proving that the oceans originated from perspiration, not rainfall. Earth strayed from the heavenly path only once. After the dance he tore up his card and forswore the antics of Venus. Since that time he has remained a sky-flower pasted to orbit, declaring to his neighbor Mars that "nothing short of an act of Comet" could make him wander from his celestial coordinates.

In contrast to Boeotian story, most tales depict Venus as lethargic.

For the annual crafts fair in Carthage, LaBelle Watrous painted Venus. LaBelle entitled her painting, "Venus De Chartres," named after, she said, the picture of Venus which Huguenots stole from the Cathedral at Chartres at the end of the sixteenth century. On LaBelle's canvas Venus slouched in a rocking chair on a front porch. In her left hand she held a red peach. She had just bitten the peach, and juice oozed over her lips and dripped down her chin. Holding a mirror in her right hand, Venus gazed at her reflection. Venus wore down-at-the-heel slippers, and her feet splayed out in front of the rocker. Between her feet a basket lay on its side, peas spilling out like water. Under the porch Sloth slept in an elbow of dirt. He wore a shiny black suit and resembled, Turlow Gutheridge said, "Hink Ruunt turned Pentecostal." In his left fist Sloth grasped a cross, his fingers clutching the gold like a ball of tobacco worms gnawing a leaf. Cradled between his right arm and his chest was a pickle jar, blue with moonshine. A menagerie of biblical creatures appeared on the canvas, just as they did in the original painting, LaBelle assured viewers. To the left of the porch steps Ribaldry perched on a red saddle atop a duck. Above his head he held a rabbit with orange antlers. At the other side of the porch stood a unicorn. Instead of pointing upward the creature's horn hung down limply, tumbling over his forelock and dangling between his front legs, looking like, Loppie Groat said, whittling words politely and referring to his mule, "Jeddry's laborer of nature."

The closest most Carthaginians ever came to a French dancing girl was Madame Fifi who performed in Adam and Eve clubs around Nashville. Even then Fifi was a stage name, and the Madame had never traveled farther from Tennessee than Rome, Georgia, much less tangoed in France. "She's a Turnipseed from Buena Vista," Loppie Groat told the crowd at Ankerrow's Café. "Her daddy was a cooper and made the best whiskey barrels in East Tennessee." Much as castor beans thrive when planted deep in the bowels of the earth, so Madame Fifi's performances sprouted green and vigorous over time, one runner evolving into massage therapy, another mutating into the escort service. Madame Fifi aged gracefully, in her fifties shifting her act from clubs to carnivals. One night in Belle Meade she fell from a trapeze and broke her right leg so badly that it had to be amputated. Fifi refused to let the doctor at Vanderbilt Hospital dispose of the leg. By the time she was afoot again flesh had fallen from the bones. From that time until her death she carried the bones wherever she went, packing them in a grip lined with voile, explaining that at the Resurrection she wanted all her limbs so she could wade the crystal river and dance along the golden streets. "Some night," she said, "I'm going to perform before the Great White Throne and make the sanctified smile." "If I kick high enough maybe the brethren will remember this lush country and happy evenings of sowing and harvesting, times before they became Christian soldiers and marched into the red din of doctrinal battle, waving bibles like swords."

Because grammar ties them to low commas and semicolons, English teachers rarely climb heights as poetic as those scaled by Madame Fifi. Still, on occasion professors will toss parentheses to the wind and kick up their heels. In January, three days before the spring semester began, Tom, Roger, Mickey, Jack, Dick, John, and I wheeled down to Colchester and ate lunch at Nu Nu's, a restaurant operated, the owner said, by Sicilian Jews. "Noted," Mickey added, elevating conversation beyond the culinary soft-shoe, "for kosher vendettas." Since the seven of us had ascended the hump of middle age and were reeling down what we hoped would be a long far slope, we were, as Vicki put it, "a chorus line, more adept at the can't-can't than the cancan." Still, despite not munching a bolero of exotic tastes, I had fun and was adventuresome, eating my first frittata, one rich with a crescendo of spinach and Italian sausage. Moreover I drank a can of Dr. Brown's Cel-Ray, soda water flavored with celery. The meal bucked us up, and afterward we drove to the Colchester Bakery and bought loaves of Russian rye bread. The girl behind the counter stared when we walked through the door. "Did you guys just get off the bus?" she asked. Once English teachers go on the town they make a day of it. From the bakery Roger directed us to Jon's Fish Market. Two picnic tables stood outside the building. "In summer, it's nice to sit at a table and eat a lobster roll and watch the traffic," Roger said. As we drove slowly through town along Hayward Street, Roger pointed out an antique store, "the best," he said, "in Colchester."

On returning home, I did not want to remove my ambling shoes, and that afternoon I went for a walk. In winter woods open, and the walker notices landmarks. I strolled along the ridge above the Ogush-witz meadow, passing Saddle Birch and Turtlehead Rock. Walking around the trunk of The Big Tree took eleven and a half long paces. At dusk the sky turned green, and a line of geese slipped across the horizon like ellipses drifting over a page. Behind the beaver pond the nest of a white-eyed vireo sagged in a sapling, and in a cold hollow frost burst from bark in splintery, white tufts. At the start of the walk I found a plastic sign on the ground. Four inches high and seven and three-quarter inches wide, the sign was yellow. Stamped in black let-ters across the top was the word WARNING, bolts of dark lightning falling jagged from both W and G. Illuminated by the lightning was the phrase "ELECTRIC FENCE." The fence, smaller letters explained, was a "Red Snap'r," manufactured by Electric Fencing Systems in Ellen-dale, Minnesota. Instead of studying the print, I should have taken the sign as an omen, warning me to put off my walk until warmer weather.

"Water is more dangerous than whiskey," Turlow Gutheridge once told me. "Thousands of people drown in water each year, but no one drowns in whiskey." Frozen water is also dangerous. Halfway down the hill behind the sheep barns, a spring percolated under the power lines. Throughout summer the path down the hill was muddy. In win-ter the water froze, and ice buckled across the slope. Usually I avoided the path until spring, but the frittata made me think I could allemande down the hill, tripping lightly from one hummock of grass to another. I was wrong. Just below the spring my feet pitched up, and I slammed backwards, my binoculars twisting behind me and between the ground and my back, in the process shattering a sheet of ice and turning two of my ribs into shards. I rolled off the ice onto my hands and knees. I couldn't stand straight. I resembled a sock, one rolled off a foot and left on the floor, as Vicki put it, "in a nerdle."

I'm not a graceful walker, and often when I return home from a walk, I drip blood or cradle an arm. Years have melted Vicki's capac-ity for sympathy. "My God!" she exclaimed when I hobbled into the kitchen. "What have you done now, you asshole?" After watching me stagger about with a cane the next day, she said, "you look just like your father." Actually the cane was useful. In the bookstore I slashed about and cleared paths, shouting, "Out of the way, Childhood. Make way for Beauty and Intelligence." In contrast to polite requests, the lexicon of youth recognizes commands, and students skipped out of my way faster than eighth notes.

My ribs throbbed. A brown pool spread across my back, my skin absorbing color like a cloth, water. Although walking was easy, standing up was difficult. At night I coiled and slithered, hissing in pain. Getting out of bed took half an hour, and for two days I ate and drank little in order to avoid the lavatory. Pain rang in castanets when I coughed and clanged like cymbals after a sneeze. In class I whispered, and smiles slid across my face as slowly as pavanes. The pain produced side effects. I experienced a loss of short-term sartorial memory. One afternoon my scarf vanished in the English department. I bought the scarf in 1963 when I was a student at Cambridge. The scarf was pink and claret, the colors those of my college, and I didn't want to lose it after thirty-four years. I searched for the scarf for forty minutes. I would have looked longer, but bending over made my ribs ache, so I limped home. "I lost my scarf," I said to Vicki, taking off my coat in the kitchen. "You did?" Vicki said, staring. "Yes," I began, then stopped, suddenly noticing the scarf around my neck. The next day when I started home from the department, I couldn't find my gloves. After twenty minutes I found them atop my head, under my stocking cap, a place I often put them while I stuff books and papers into cloth bags.

The most noticeable side effect of pain was irritability. One night Eliza and I watched television together. A program compared education in China with that in the United States. Students in China learned more facts than students in the United States, a high school principal in Massachusetts conceded. "But our boys and girls are more creative," he said. "How many Chinese win a Pulitzer prize?" he asked. "Daddy," Eliza said looking puzzled. "I thought Pulitzer prizes were only awarded in America." "That's right," I said. "Well, then," Eliza continued, "how can Chinese win them?" "They can't," I said, snapping off the television. "The principal is an absolute kazoo." I reacted strongly because the man's remark came at the end of a toccata of irritants that began early that morning when a student said, "Have an enhanced day." In response I almost quoted Tennessee Williams, attaching an item found in toolboxes, the metallic companion of nuts, bolts, and nails, to the word *you*. Although the boy's lexicon would have recognized the phrase, I smothered the remark, so tightening chest and temptation that my ribs felt as if claves were playing across them.

"Nine weeks," a doctor said at one of Eliza's basketball games. "You will feel better after nine weeks." Thirty-one days have passed, and I am still irritable. Last week I spoke in Farmington at a fundraiser for the university. To avoid potholes and jarring my ribs, I drove slowly. As cars churned past, one of Josh's remarks came to mind. "People in the fast lane," he said, "are going nowhere. They have already broken down and have been left behind on the shoulder of life." Twice this past fortnight I spoke for the university. As honoraria I received a hokey-pokey of things: a mug, a key chain, and one and a half cups of coffee, the first cup with cream, the second half without. Vicki once said that Mother told her I laughed the day I was born. In the past when given mugs, sweat shirts, and bottles of vintage vinegar masquerading as champagne, I smiled. This January good humor made me wince. "Three days to prepare a speech, and five hours driving, and not even a cookie," I muttered.

To be truthful a cacophony of moods rang through each day. Years ago I thought writing would increase the tempo of my life. Instead writing has slowed my doings to a half-note. Recently Oprah Winfrey discussed a friend's book on television. The next week the book sat atop the best-seller list. "Royalties from my eleven books," I told Vicki, "bring me $8.06 a week, or $1.1514 a day, not enough to buy two cups of coffee each morning at the Cup of Sun." Vicki did not answer me. Instead she went to the attic. Fifteen minutes later she walked into the study, carrying a small Victorian wall-hanging. The hanging was fifteen inches long and six inches wide. At each end of the hanging a rose bush was red with blossoms. The bushes functioned as book ends, supporting the phrase, "GIVE ME A CENT, MOTHER."

The mazurka on the hill having ruptured the boiler of my locomotive skills, I have spent most days since the spill in the house with books. One day I selected forty-four volumes to donate to the annual sale at the Mansfield Library. While twenty-five of the books had been published in the '90s and thirteen in the '80s, only two had been published in the '70s, three in the '60s, and two in the '50s. These last two volumes were reprints of books I won't read again, Ford Madox Ford's *The Good Soldier* and William Faulkner's *The Sound and the Fury,* tales that darken even black nights. Essays I wrote appeared in four books. Authors mentioned me in three additional books, one man describing a dinner party I attended at his house. For two books I had written puffs, ignoring the slow beat of paragraphs and labeling pastorales, intellectual gallops. Six of the books were gifts inscribed by their authors. The more extravagant an inscription the quicker I donate the book to the library. "Whoever buys this book will see the inscription and realize that I am a person of consequence," I said to Vicki, showing her a paragraph praising me.

Stature being a matter more of perception than achievement, I inscribed several books to myself. "For Sam Pickering, America's Montaigne," I wrote. "Every night I pray to the literary deities—Milton, Shakespeare, and the apostle Matthew—begging them to bless me with talent like yours. Even they genuflect before your achievement. *Ecce Quam Bonum.*" "How can you write such stuff?" Vicki asked. "Sometimes," I said, quoting Turlow Gutheridge, "you have to act the ass to get the bran."

Because flying makes me more nervous now than in the past, I rarely leave Connecticut, and only one of the forty-four books was airplane reading, John Le Carre's thriller *Our Game.* As my interests change, so do the books on my shelves. Years ago I swept two score books devoted to Charles Dickens from the house. This year I jettisoned children's books and studies which described childhood: fairy tales, novels, and school texts. Pitching books makes me feel lightheaded, much as I do after giving blood. When I was not pruning the library or teaching, I spent days in bed reading, hoping quiet signatures of pages would set my ribs. Books may cure ailments of the mind, particularly ennui, but they do nothing for the body. Nevertheless, I read memoirs of naturalists, dreaming that descriptions of field and wood might roll across me like the conga and invigorate Nature. I swallowed a book a day and didn't waste time simmering paragraphs for decoctions or pulping sentences for poultices, among other volumes reading Frank Bolles's *Land of the Lingering Snow. Chronicles of a Stroller in New England from January to June* (1891), *According to Season. Talks about Flowers in Order of Their Appearance in the Woods and Fields*

(1894) by Mrs. William Starr Dana, and *Naturalist at Large* (1944), the memoirs of Thomas Barbour, director of the Agassiz Museum at Harvard. I studied the reactions of earlier readers. Only one passage in John Muir's *The Story of My Boyhood and Youth* (1913) was underlined. When a boy, Muir left Scotland and moved to a farm in Wisconsin. On page sixty-three of the memoir, Muir celebrated the change. "Without knowing it," he hymned, and a reader underlined in pencil, "we were still at school; every wild lesson a love lesson, not whipped but charmed into us. Oh, that glorious Wisconsin wilderness!"

Readers did not react to several books. On the title page of *Land of the Lingering Snow* appeared the inscription, "Helen from Judith." Helen was not much stroller, at least not through books. Many pages of Bolles's book were uncut, the first example occurring after page nine, the tenth and eleventh pages sealed from sight. Occasionally packaging raised my spirits more than content. Clarence Moores Weed dedicated *Ten New England Blossoms and Their Insect Visitors* (1895) to his child, writing, "For My Little Daughter Irene, For Me The Most Charming Of New England Blossoms." On the leaf opposite the dedication appeared a photograph of Irene. Four years old, Irene wore a long dress, so puffed and gathered at the shoulders that she seemed a swelling bud. Loose curls of brown hair unraveled like calyxes over Irene's forehead. In her hands Irene held a small book resembling a Psalter. Two Easter lilies were rooted in the crook of her left arm, the blossoms rising in white horns over her shoulder and the stems sliding across her side like leafy ceremonial ribbons. I saunter aisles of libraries, and much as the walker finds medicinal plants at the edges of fields, so I stumbled upon most of the books. The only book I sought out was Raymond L. Ditmars's *The Making of a Scientist* (1937). Ditmars was a herpetologist, and in the 1950s, I read his books. In summers I roamed my grandfather's farm in Virginia, catching turtles, lizards, and snakes, my imagination transforming black and hog-nosed snakes into bushmasters, Gaboon vipers, and fer-de-lances.

Despite the regimen of books, my ribs remained venomously sore. In contrast to its effect on health, however, reading influenced writing. *The Making of a Scientist* brought Carthage to mind. The inhabitants of Boot and One-Eye, two malarial coves below Carthage, ate poisonous snakes in order to protect themselves against mosquitoes.

Expelled through sweat glands, the venom collected on people's skins with the result that almost as soon as a mosquito lit on an inhabitant of either cove, the insect slumped over dead. Although pharmacological studies could not determine the relative effectiveness of eating various snakes, the citizens of Boot chewed copperheads exclusively while those in One-Eye devoured water moccasins. Local churches distributed snakes on Sundays, and time transformed differences in diet from the culinary and the prophylactic to the spiritual. As a result people living in Boot refused to speak to folks in One-Eye. "The apple of discord tempted them, and they did eat the serpent," Turlow Gutheridge said.

Foolish doings in Carthage are my Folies-Bergères. Instead of painted ladies, a painted coffin was toast of the town. To honor Civil War dead, the Tabernacle of Love sponsored an "Obsequial Festival" at the Pillow of Heaven Cemetery. Because the graveyard was new, no Confederate soldiers were buried in it. To add body to the festival Slubey Garts sent Proverbs Goforth to Shiloh. Late at night Proverbs dug up two wheelbarrows of dirt from The Hornet's Nest, soil, he said, bound to contain blood and bone, fears and hopes. One Sunday after church Slubey Garts buried the dirt in the graveyard. Although the Fairy Minstrels of Dorcas played flutes beside the grave, the coffin in which Proverbs shoveled the dirt was the talk of the ceremony.

On the top of the coffin Isom Legg painted a picture of the first day's battle at Shiloh. At the foot of the coffin stood the Shiloh Church. Around it wound Purdy and Eastern and Western Corinth roads. Bloody Pond glistened above the middle of the coffin. To the left of the pond was the Peach Orchard, Albert Sidney Johnson lying on his back in a red pool. At the head of the coffin flowed the Tennessee River, two gunboats, the *Tyler* and the *Lexington*, firing cannons, smoke rising from their barrels like gray hair. Capillaries of blue and gray corpuscles washed over the upper half of the coffin, Sherman on the River Road along the right side, Benjamin Prentiss's abandoned camp along the left. After seeing the coffin, several Carthaginians hired Isom for paint jobs, the most memorable being a sign with a whale on the front, painted for Zibetheum Hooberry, the plumber. "Because a whale got a prophet out of water," Zibetheum explained, referring to Jonah, "the whale is the patron animal of plumbers."

I had just begun to consider the whale's flukes when Vicki walked into the study. "How is the choreography for the corps de ballet?" she asked, alluding to the French dancing girls. Vicki thinks me a low paragraphist, and our conversational pas de deux lack lift and invariably resemble schottisches. "I have not framed jetés and turns," I said. "But I have selected a danseuse or two." "Who?" Vicki asked, not quite able to follow my verbal bourrées. "I'm glad you asked," I said, thinking myself not simply a ballet but a word master. "Alabama Girl, Cotton-Eyed Jo, Bunny Hop, Darling Nellie Gray, Katy Hill, and Pattycake Polka." I thought the list of dancers would render Vicki as speechless as one of the Wilis. I underestimated her. For a moment Vicki was silent. But then she clapped her hands together and skipped out the door, singing "Hinky-Dinky Parlez-Vous."

At Odds

I'm irritable in February. Rain and snow confine me to the house, and the vague discontents that nag me during the rest of the year sharpen into focus. One morning I wrote a letter urging the state legislature to name the chickadee state bird. The moment had arrived, I wrote, to boot the aristocratic incumbent, the cardinal, off the perch. Not only did the chickadee reside year round in Connecticut, but unlike the elitist, suburban cardinal, the chickadee did not demand an estate ranging from three to ten acres. A friendly democrat, the chickadee enjoyed neighbors, and a flock of birds shared a territory. That afternoon I wrote a politician, telling her to stop thrashing about in the poisonous sumac and ivy of campaign reform. "Act constructively," I wrote, "and propose goldenrod as the national flower." "From shore to shore goldenrod waves yellow. In bogs and swamps, across prairies and along roadsides, in fields and over hills, through woods and thickets, goldenrod blooms," I said, "its flowers composed of scores of minute florets, illustrating that in some unions there is strength, rather than rancorous, debilitating ethnicity." The next day my discontent shifted from birds and flowers to superficial matters. At noon on the radio I called the new president of the university a hologram. Later at a meeting of the university senate a vice president said an ethics committee was not needed to police brick-and-mortar contracts. "Right," I said. "Establishing an ethics committee would be fatuous, particularly since no one in administration knows what ethics are." "What's next?" Vicki said that night at dinner. "February has just begun."

What came next was a walk. The more I avoid people, the better I think them, at least in February. Atop silos by the sheep barn, pigeons huddled together in fleecy skullcaps. Starlings forced an ash out of season. A flock rustled across limbs like compound leaves, song flapping about them almost as if a ragged paper roll had been crammed into a player piano. Below the barn lay vats of silage wrapped in white plastic. The silage fermented and oozed through holes in the plastic, the fragrance sifting into the breeze like bourbon seeping through water. Turkeys foraged along the edge of the field beside the barbed-wire fence. Beneath barberry lay secondary feathers torn from a blue jay. As I leaned over to look at the feathers, juncos blew out of the barberry, rising lightly like a sheet of burnt paper, then breaking and falling into tatters of white and gray ash. At the beginning of the walk the sky resembled a charcoal sketch. As shades of gray and blue blurred into brown, they smoothed trees out of clarity, ironing knots out of pitch pine and pressing olive and alder back into scrub.

A winter wren bounced between a stone wall and Kessel Creek. Ice had jerked debris from the dam in the woods. Tighter than an absorbent green bandage, liverwort stretched across the remaining stones. Beside a tread made by the wheel of a mountain bike lay a packet which once contained one and one-tenth ounces of GU Vanilla Bean, a "Fast Food For Athletes" manufactured in Berkeley, California. Walking tired me, and in hopes of discovering something that would make me tread lightly, I scanned the ingredients. Only a pharmacist could decipher the contents: "Maltodextrin, Filtered Water, Fructose, Leucine, Pectin, Valine, Potassium and Sodium Citrate, Histidine, Sea Salt, Calcium Carbonate, Potassium Sorbate and Benzoate As Preservatives, Calcium Chloride, GU Herbal Blend™: [Astragalus, Chamomile, Cola Nut Extract (Has Caffeine), Ginseng]. Bourbon Vanilla, GU Antioxidant Blend™: [Beta Carotene, Vitamin C, Vitamin E], Citric Acid." Instructions urged gourmands to drink "a few mouthfuls of water" after eating GU. Unfortunately I could not wash the ingredients down with my vocabulary. Even if I swished them around in a brew akin to that in the silage, I couldn't swallow the words.

More palatable to my lexicographical taste were carvings stenciled into the trunk of a beech near the dam. For a decade I'd noticed the carvings, but not until the GU stuck to my cerebrum did I slow down and read the bark. A filigree of names scrolled around the tree: Bumble, Rap, Rich, and Seno. While joining KW to MD produced a mysterious result, the product probably resembled that of the addition of Cheryl to Ken and Shan to Jen. Not only was CW an active man about town, but he was a philandering carver as well, linking himself to RP in 1932 then the next year to Joy, this last coupling enclosed within a heart. In 1988 the woods were host to a Venusian festival, as nine couples carved their initials in the bark. The celebration must have been a success, for in 1989 fourteen couples added their names to the tree. Despite the fecundity of the two gatherings, the rite did not become an annual event. In 1990 Venus must have swung into superior conjunction. Drifting out of sight, then mind, she no longer transformed sharp dealings into soft, amorous dallyings.

From the beech a grove of saplings spread back through the woods like words falling down a page under a title. Buds on saplings resembled wicks, orange but not yet warm enough to flame into leaf. On the ridge above the Fenton River, icicles slid off rocks, tapering and stretching until they touched the ground and their tips spread, swelling like sprained ankles. Tiles of ice lay on the banks of the Fenton, tossed above the water by the cutting and slicing of a February thaw. A stump jutted out from the bank. Beneath it at water's edge bony roots knitted bales of twig and branch into thatch. At the feet of trees, snow melted and froze, gathering lumpy under dark arches. Amid moss purling and doubling over rotten logs, small stone flies winked, their wings thin as tracery.

Turning away from the river, I walked across the Ogushwitz meadow. Carpenter ants chewed the heartwood of an oak into wainscoting. In a hole abandoned by a woodpecker lurked the remains of a bird's nest, a broken cup of grass, leaves, bark, and fur. Suddenly, the sun washed charcoal out of the sky. Above the raspberry patch, branches of staghorn sumac curved up like wrought iron, their tips scarlet with fruit. As the light turned through the hour, it pulled not simply the colorful but the indistinct into vision. Beside the pumping station a deer jacker had cleaned and gutted a doe. The man drove a pickup truck with wide tires. The back wheels sank in the soggy ground while he butchered the deer, tossing the hide and entrails against the fence.

At sunset colors broke across the day, baking the sky into agateware, the jagged bands first crisp then losing definition and flowing milky. Life is too various for a person to remain at odds with any time of the year, especially after a walk. The next day I went to the Wadsworth Atheneum in Hartford, the sunset seeming to draw me after it through the horizon toward light, particularly to galleries containing the American Impressionists and the Hudson River school of painters. For a long time I stared at George Inness's *Autumn Gold*. Nuggets of light flickered through trees then slid across a meadow into a silver stream. A silky mist slipped down Albert Bierstadt's *In the Mountains*, catching on bluffs turning their surfaces soft, Vicki said later, "as sentimental prose."

Long after memory hardens, prose remains sentimental. One evening a vase of roses appeared on the kitchen table. "They are a Valentine's present from you," Vicki said. "There's a bit of Don Juan in the old boy yet," I said, sitting down. "Sometimes I surprise myself. But where did I buy the flowers and what did I pay for them?" "At the Horticultural Salesroom for twelve dollars," Vicki said. "You went there because the gardener follows the European custom of giving an uneven number of roses, thirteen stems in a dozen instead of twelve." On President's Day I did better. I drove the Toyota to Willi Lube. Many people's thoughts having run to oil and crankcase rather than to Lincoln and Washington, the waiting room was crowded. For a while I sat on a chair with a green plastic bottom and watched dust sift through sunlight. Crumpled on the table next to me was the sports section of *USA Today*, but I didn't read it. Instead I walked two doors down Main Street and bought a half-dozen doughnuts at Dunkin' Donuts: an apple doughnut for Francis, chocolate for both Eliza and Edward, and for Vicki, three creams—Boston, vanilla, and chocolate.

That afternoon I attended the Connecticut State 4-H Poultry Show. The Poultry Science Club at the university staged the show in the Ratcliffe-Hicks Arena. The floor of the arena was oval and resembled a flattened egg, fresh sawdust billowing across it thick as cream. On the side of the arena opposite the entrance a large slab of white-washed plywood leaned against a wall. Painted in the middle of the board was the head of a Single Comb Light Brown Leghorn. The bird's ear and bill were yellow. Its comb and wattles were scarlet, and brown feathers tipped with gold swept rakishly down its back. Curving over the comb in a blue dome were the words "Connecticut State 4-H." Ruffling under the bird's neck was "Poultry Show." Sod had been laid around the board, and a small garden swept out from the bottom of the slab, rocks forming an ornamental border, two small blue spruce trees standing like gates on each side. The floor of the arena was divided into halves. To the right was the exhibition area, furnished with two short rows of tables. To the left stretched four rows of cafeteria tables, each row consisting of four tables. Two lines of square wire cages containing chickens ran down each row. Sawdust covered the bottoms of the cages, and paper cups filled with water were attached to hooks on sides. Crammed under tables were "Pet Taxis." At the south end of the arena was a miscellany of birds: English Call ducks; three Brown China geese, all barking; a turkey; and then "Raffle Birds." Spectators could buy chances on flocks of birds, among others, a Light Brown Leghorn hen with two chicks, bantam Buff Cochins; a bantam White Crested Black Polish, two Old English chicks, and five Blue Cochin chicks. I considered buying a ticket. Unlike me, though, Vicki does not appreciate live chickens, and winning would have upset the domestic roost, provoking squabbling and ending with my being skewered if not fricasseed.

Poster boards lined part of the wall of the arena. In the 1950s the Poultry Club was called the Bankiva Club after *gallus bankiva*, the jungle fowl supposedly an ancestor of the chicken. One board described diseases of chickens. Printed beneath the symptoms of diseases were pictures of ailing chickens. Below Newcastle Disease a hatchery of white chickens sprawled unplucked in the dirt. The wattles of a bird suffering from Fowl Cholera resembled brown paper grocery bags damp and rotten with garbage. After sampling the cavortings of round and tape worms, my appetite for pictures, particularly for those spicy with vermiform seasoning, waned. Indeed the photograph of a tangle of hairworms having made my scalp itch, I pushed such garnishes out of sight and hurried off to watch Junior Novices exhibit their birds.

Both boys and girls, the exhibitors ranged from eight to twelve years old. All wore white shirts and white ties, the latter usually string ties as thin as hairworms. Three girls painted their lips so red that their mouths resembled combs, and two extended their eyebrows so far down their cheeks that their brows fluttered when they smiled. Pinned on the shoulders of each contestant was a placard, supplied by Blue Seal Feeds and with a number stamped upon it. Beside the number was the logo of the company, a blue rosette. "Mark of Quality Since 1868," small print at the bottom of the placard explained. After putting their birds into cages, the exhibitors turned and faced a long table covered with white paper. At the judge's command they fetched their birds, pulling them out of the cages head first so feathers would not be ruffled. After having turned back around, the exhibitors pushed their chickens under their right arms, pinning them against their sides, making certain that the birds' heads pointed back toward the cages while spreading the tails so that they faced the spectators and resembled feather dusters. The judge then examined the cages to be sure doors were shut, saying "foxes can't pull chickens out of closed cages." Next the judge put contestants through their paces, instructing them, for example, to show the birds' right wings, "depth of body," and pubic and breast bones. He also asked the children to walk their birds around the table. To control their animals, exhibitors rested their left hands on the backs of the birds. Nevertheless, several chickens escaped, one perching on the top rail of a wooden gate and three others flopping to the floor and scratching through the sawdust. When a Black Rose Comb refused to walk and hunkered down on the paper, his owner pushed him forward so he skied along the table.

I stayed at the show for two hours, spending most of the time looking at chickens, marveling at the variety: Silver Leghorns, Creoles, Partridge Wyandottes, Golden Campines, Barred and Partridge Plymouth Rocks, Dark Brahmas, elegant Gold Sebrights, and Silver Sebrights, rhapsodies in black and white. While Buff Cochins resembled small dogs with their hair teased into feathers, White Wyandottes looked like big snowballs. A knob of feathers sprocketed out of the head of a Black Crested White Polish, and gold and silver feathers tumbled like water down the back of a Belgian Booted Porcelain, transforming the bird into a pastel pitcher. While feathers rumpled around the legs of a Millefleur, turning its feet into mops, Black Silkies themselves resembled dust mops, friendly mops, the kind that would not destroy the webs of house spiders. Old English birds were popular, and exhibitors showed several varieties, my favorite being the Wheaten, a small jug-sized bird the color of newly harvested grain.

I enjoyed the show. The cackling and scratching raised my spirits, and for two days afterward, I ignored gray skies, and behaved, as Vicki put it, "like a good egg." The egg comparison aside, rarely do I hatch plans in February. Instead addled repetition entertains me. During a midterm examination I studied the class, much as I did last February. Of the thirty-three students, five were left-handed, and four wore glasses. During the test two boys drank coffee while six girls wore scrunchies. Five of the girls wore them on their heads while one right-handed girl wore her scrunchy on her left wrist. During the test several students coughed, but only one suffered from plugged nostrils, causing her to wheeze and snort. Five boys and two girls wore baseball caps, two of the boys wearing them backwards. Thirty-eight minutes into the test one boy removed his hat and dropped it on the floor, in hopes, I suppose, of airing his brain so he could think better.

For many people the activities of one February rarely differ from those of the next February. Forced inside the house, they pass time writing letters. Not only do I write letters about plants and animals, but I receive more letters in February than I receive during any other month of the year. Early in the month a man wrote from Delaware, asking me to assess a poem written by his daughter, an eighth grader. The girl wrote the poem one morning during mathematics class. Later that day she showed the poem to her English teacher. When the teacher did not praise the poem lavishly, the girl was upset. "Please be as objective as you can and let her know what you think about her poem," the father wrote. "She needs your support at this time." Entitled "Sad," the poem began, "Sad tree. Sad house. / Spinning flowers in my life." The remaining ten lines did not contribute much more to the poem. That afternoon I wrote the girl, studiously trying to avoid saying something her father could use to criticize the English teacher. "Your father sent me a copy of your poem 'Sad.' You have a nice lyric touch, and the piece is soft and gentle," I began. "But I will tell you what I tell students at the university. You have made a beginning, but you must push on." I suggested to the girl that she read several collections of poetry. "Writing," I said, "does not come easily. My friends who publish poetry often revise their poems thirty or forty times. Poetry is more a matter of work—hard, slogging work—than inspiration." Lastly, I wished the girl good luck then described something silly I did on the athletic rather than the poetic field when I was thirteen years old.

From Indiana a woman wrote and described her childhood. Raising two children taxed the woman's mother. "When Momma got tired," the woman said, "she went into the back yard and sat in the car. She locked the doors and turned the car around so that it faced the sun. Then she slumped forward and rested her head on the steering wheel. After a while Johnny and I usually went outside and climbed on to the hood of the car. We pressed our faces against the windshield. Sometimes after looking up, Momma unlocked the car door and took us back to the house. Other times she turned on the wipers and slumped back over."

Two people sent me folktales. A Virginian declared that he was a man after my tooth, adding that although his story "might cause the occipital plugatorial bonums of the dull to ache like root canals," he thought I'd fancy the tale. According to my correspondent, a countryman unearthed a giant copperhead while digging up his garden in the spring. Before the man chopped the snake's head off, the serpent bit the wooden handle of the shovel. During winter the snake's venom sacks had filled with poison, and soon after being bit, the handle of the shovel started swelling. Eventually the handle grew as big as the trunk of a large oak. The man then carted it to a sawmill and turned the handle into enough lumber to build the finest outhouse in Hanover County, "spacious as a department store" and not just a waxing moon ornamenting the door but a full moon complete with a shade and then a horizon of constellations, Camelopardalis, Musca, Cepheus, and Cassiopeia. One evening, however, as the proud owner perched "in the emporium" pondering zodiacal doings, the poison lost its virulence and the boards began to shrink. The lumber shrank so fast that the "owner did not have time to pull up his trousers." As the boards collapsed, they pushed the "man down the hole of the privy." Bent double like a safety pin, the man got stuck near the bottom of the hole. "He was so impacted that no one could free him." The local gold-finder attempted unsuccessfully to pry him loose with a crowbar, and a well digger failed to hoist him up with a rig of pulleys. Eventually "a member of a medical lodge" poured twenty gallons of castor oil down the privy and blasted the man out of the hole. "The explosion was so great," the letter stated, "that fields ten miles away on the other side of Ashland received a dressing of fertilizer." On the top floor of the Jefferson Hotel in Richmond, a weatherman saw the blast, and thinking it a tornado, rushed downstairs and, interrupting a gospel show on the radio, urged Richmonders to dive into their cellars and stay there until the tempest passed. "All that hullabaloo for just an old shit storm," the mayor said later as he climbed out of his basement, brushing crickets out of his hair. The man himself landed in the Pamunkey River. Once he finished scrubbing, he drove to Ashland and ordered an indoor flush toilet from the Sears-Roebuck catalogue.

A woman living in south Alabama described a murder. In her county, she recounted, a thief once stole more cotton than did the boll weevil. Although neighbors suspected a particular man, they couldn't prove him guilty. Then one summer the man went too far. Surprised while stealing, he killed a young farmer. Because the crime occurred at night and no one saw the murder, the sheriff couldn't arrest the man. "Once again," my correspondent wrote, "people thought evil would escape punishment." The townsfolk had not reckoned on the farmer's wife, however, thinking her too occupied with a new, unweaned baby to avenge her husband. On the advice of a faith doctor, the wife did not bury her husband until six days after his death when a small white maggot crawled out of his right nostril. Immediately the wife began to breast feed the grub. Fastened to her bosom, the creature lapped up milk. On the fourth day the worm released its hold on the woman's breast. Bluish-green and as big as a spaniel, the creature crawled out of the house and vanished. Eight days later the body of the murderer was found leaning against a barn. While the man's head pressed against the barn, his feet splayed out behind him. A web of silk threads tied the man's head to the wood and his feet to the ground. The man's skin was yellow, and his body a hollow shell, his insides having been sucked out through a hole the size of a fist just below his liver. Under the man's body hung a hammock of silk, the sort of "roof" the grub of a gigantic chalcis fly might build, an entomologist concluded. For the next twenty years chalcis flies swarmed over the widow's fields killing parasites. As a result the widow harvested bumper crops and became "the most successful cotton farmer south of Wetumpka."

Most people who write me have read my books. Often such people tell stories about characters who stroll through my essays. In February a man in Knoxville, Tennessee, wrote and asked if I'd run across Lanthorne Cokes on any of my narrative journeys. Known familiarly as Wasp, Cokes was a beggar by day and a moon man by night, "a gentleman of the shade" who burgled pigpens and chicken coops. For years Wasp plied his trades in Tennessee. "He owned more costumes than a circus clown and changed clothes and personalities whenever he migrated to a different town." Wasp's most famous character was a deformed beggar. A thin man, Wasp often sat by a road with one of his legs bent under him. He wore a nightshirt that spread across the ground, hiding his folded leg. The other leg jutted out in front of him. Accompanying Wasp on his travels was an abattoir of animal parts. Alongside the real leg he placed an artificial leg. Sometimes Wasp wrapped a bandage around the fibula and tibia of a deer. He left the hoof attached and arranged the bones so that they stuck out under his shirt. Once or twice he got hold of a ham rotten with maggots and after forcing a shoe over the hock used the ham as a leg.

I'd never met Wasp. My correspondent's letter, however, brought to mind Carthage, Tennessee, a place I visited often at the end of February when days were cold and drab. Above Guess Creek just beyond Bone Camp, a pentecostal congregation moved into an abandoned farm house. The church called itself Pilgrim Rest Here. Beside the front door of the house two automobile head lamps sat atop posts. Big and silver, the lamps, the Reverend Mathuzalum Gubby said, had once adorned a Cord automobile. "Or ever the silver cord be loosed," he said, pointing to the lamps and quoting *Ecclesiastes*. The inside of the church was bare. A homemade pulpit rested on a low slab. Clapped together from oddments of a pine sawed down behind the farmhouse, the pulpit oozed resin. For its part the slab consisted of two-by-fours six feet long joined together by dowels. On the wall behind the pulpit hung a large whole-cloth quilt decorated with flowers. In the center of the quilt Christ's crown of thorns bloomed with roses, peonies, and daisies. Cotton batting had been inserted into the back of the quilt so that the crown protruded and seemed "to bloom like the Resurrection," Mathuzalum said.

Unlike the flowers, Mathuzalum did not appear fresh from the garden. He had once been a farmer, growing cotton near Tibbie, Alabama. Unfortunately he had not enjoyed success comparable to that of the widow. Indeed the call to preach reached him one humid summer day as he was ditching a field. "The sun, not the Father, telephoned Mathuzalum," Turlow Gutheridge said in Ankerrow's Café. "Mathuzalum was born lazy and suffered a relapse." Mathuzalum was tall and skinny, and his arms were thin as hoe handles. Watery and pale blue, his eyes resembled skim milk. Time having ploughed his farming days into the past, his hands were soft as carpet slippers, and his skin appeared bleached, so much so that his freckles looked white. In contrast Mathuzalum's wife Zaidee was short and fatter than a mole. Unlike her "lower half" who traipsed after the divine afflatus stumbling into verbal inelegancies such as bumblebee cotton and peckerwood corn, Zaidee was extraordinarily proper. Never did she sink to common utterance, referring, for example, to bulls as cows' husbands.

As Lanthorne Cokes mastered the sartorial arts, so Mathuzalum was ringmaster to a menagerie of sounds. During a sermon Mathuzalum hooted, mewed, whistled like a dove, grunted like an alligator, fell on his hands and knees and barked then jumped up and bayed like a coonhound suffering from infected adenoids. Whatever Mathuzalum did, however, his preaching was effective, especially on Holy Ghost Nights. By the end of a sermon almost all the congregation had been "slain in the spirit" and was outside the church rolling on the grass, speaking the heavenly language, or, as Turlow put it, "hemorrhaging syllables." When a theologian from the Harvard Theological School asked Mathuzalum to describe his "methodology," Mathuzalum said he simply "launched his sermons into the fountain filled with blood." "Pitched inside and out with the nectar of Christ's tears," the seams of faith were "gospel-tight." "Hewn with the rough ax of sanctified living," his sermons, he declared, weren't painted "like Jezebel or hung with banners like those of some Baptist pontiff."

Most pilgrims who sailed with Mathuzalum were, in Turlow's words, "poor as gully dirt." For them celestial winds blew through the sermons reassuringly. After Adam and Eve ate themselves out of house and home, Mathuzalum said, they followed the Lord's instructions right down to the old jot and tittle and were as fruitful as the multiplication tables, "all the way out to the number twelve times twelve." One Armistice Day the Lord paid the couple a surprise visit. While they served Him cornbread and goldenrod honey, He asked to meet their children. Ashamed of the size of her family, Eve locked most of the children in the barn and introduced Yahweh, as they called Him now that they knew Him better, to a select few of her offspring. After eating a plate of manna cake cooked with sweet buttermilk, the Lord felt well-disposed toward Eve, and He blessed the children. Instead of having to earn livings with shovels and hoes, the children would become, He assured Eve, high falutin' artists and lawyers, bankers and college professors with tenure.

Adam said Eve's manna cake was "absolutely divine and almost as irresistible as sin." Eve's offspring inherited their father's appetites, and when the aroma of cake wafted through the barn, Cleophas picked the lock on the door. Just as the Lord was stepping into His golden chariot, preparing to nip up the Rainbow Highway back to the White Throne, a horde of children raced around the porch of the farmhouse. Nits roosted in the children's hair, and the clumps of straw and manure between their toes looked like robins' nests. At first the Lord thought the children a variety of possum. "Created by that mischievous baby Jesus," he told Michael later, "some morning when I slept in after a night of sampling grapes."

After Cleophas licked the bottom of the cake dish, the Lord realized the creatures were almost human. Not believing that they could ever be scrubbed into the presentable, He made them servants and workers, farmers, "folks like us," Mathuzalum said, "who don't trust banks but who keep their awls in their hands or under the mattress." "But," Mathuzalum continued, "our time is nigh. Our combs are turning red. Don't worry about the goneness of the past. It won't be long now, as the monkey said when his tail got caught in the meat grinder."

For generations, Mathuzalum explained, Eve's other children had worn suits. Because they dressed themselves up like sore fingers, the infection of the world had spread from cuticle and bank account to the soul. Not once since they wrapped cotton shirts about their hearts had the favored children walked in the sunshine of faith or slathered themselves with the healthy anointment of God's salvation. In contrast the servants and farmers worked hard and having learned to tote and carry were ready to become masters. "If the ax is missing when the time comes to kill the goose," Mathuzalum declared, "we don't worry none. We just saw the head off."

"You might as well try to teach a worm to dance on its tail as expect Mathuzalum to talk sense," Proverbs Goforth said after Loppie Groat mentioned the sermon in Ankerrow's Café. Mathuzalum's success provoked Proverbs. Earlier during the week two Carthaginians had forsaken Slubey Garts and the Tabernacle of Love and had dived, as Proverbs said, "soul and appendicitis into Mathuzalum's bushmeeting religion." Proverbs himself grew corn and tobacco, and he resented the insinuation that pentecostals handled animals better than people belonging to other churches. When Slubey Garts was a little baby, Proverbs said, he baptized a rattlesnake, converting it to a rat snake. "Slubey didn't stop with dousing the snake in the creek," Proverbs said. "He cared for that serpent soul and body. So the snake would not fall back into poisonous ways, he appointed him head mouser in his daddy's barn." Later when he was just a boy, Proverbs continued, Slubey practiced preaching in his father's chicken house. The bible corn was so good, Proverbs said, that the hens all became Christians. As a result they laid eggs with single yolks from Monday through Friday. On Saturday they laid eggs with double yolks so that on Sunday they would not profane the Sabbath with work.

A partisan in the Grand Army of the Lord, Proverbs occasionally stretched the truth in theological skirmishes. When Mathuzalum's congregation sponsored a supper, Proverbs accused the church of serving mule, "tough railway mule, not even levee or sugar mule," he said. According to Proverbs, barbecued mule heads with honeydew melons between their teeth decorated the tables. To the lunchtime crowd Proverbs read a list of dishes served at the supper. The menu was sophisticated, and rumor said Turlow Gutheridge cooked it up.

Be that as it may, however, the meal began with Mulegatawny Soup followed by Potted Tongue in Aspic à la Bray. Pilgrims could choose among several dishes for main courses: Braised Mule Butt with Cabbage; Breaded Gaskin served with Grits; Withers stuffed with Okra and Wild Rice; Pickled Hooves; Sweet and Sour Pastern; and Breast of Mule atop a Bed of Sweet Potatoes, Squash, and Beefsteak Tomatoes. For sophisticated diners platters of Mule Montmorency and Mule Tartar Pomphagi were also available.

"Parboiled. If you must eat mule, be sure it is parboiled. That's the way people on Beacon Hill in Boston serve mule," my friend Josh said, after I described the church supper. "Still, no matter how mule is skinned and seasoned," he continued, "I prefer oysters." Josh had just returned to Storrs from lecturing in Massachusetts, and he had seen things he thought would interest me, in Cambridge, for example, a sign advertising a Christian Podiatrist, declaring, "I Heal." At a white-tie dinner in Framingham, a man introduced Josh to a woman he said was his "identical twin sister." Eels were served at the meal. The banker sitting next to Josh refused to eat them, explaining that he had "lost" his taste for eels ever since his father drowned. "When the Coast Guard fished Daddy out of the water," the man said, "he was awash with eels, from the roof of his mouth to the floor of his basement."

At dinner Josh does not limit himself to Adam's Ale. Consequently his stories are suspect, and his judgment is not always reliable. Beacon Hill, he said, was one of those places where a man praises his neighbors then locks his doors. After describing his trip, Josh urged me to write a letter to the *Hartford Courant*, "just like the one you wrote about the chickadees." Recently trustees of the university decided to appoint faculty representatives to each of their committees. Unfortunately, from Josh's point of view, the trustees also decided not to allow the representatives to vote. "Wheedle, cajole, beg, weep, and gnash teeth. That's what the representatives will have to do. Being a faculty member on one of those committees would be like being the only steer in a paddock of bulls. Instead of mooing and pawing, the fellow will have to park his tenderloins against the fence and clap a hoof down over his"—and here Josh used a word I'd rather not print, the word being spelled, however, just the same as that parent of a mule which is not a horse. In any case I refused to write the letter, saying, "the cowardly coon keeps his skin." Moreover March had arrived. March and zeal don't mix well, and the discontents that kicked up their heels in February had almost been broken to discretion. On the first of March Turlow wrote me from Carthage and described the weather in Smith County. One morning after a hot night, he recounted, the temperature dropped quickly, freezing the water in his pond so fast that early in the afternoon the ice was still warm.

March

Spring came late to Connecticut, and March was wintry. As soon as February ended, though, I began to dream about greenery. Moods blustered, and I forced change upon the month, imagining my restlessness reflected in bud and on wing. Around the feeders birds seemed more aggressive. One morning a nuthatch and a titmouse landed on opposite sides of the suet. Instead of ignoring the titmouse, the nuthatch shrugged his wings high over his back and then leaning forward thrust his head over the suet, so disturbing his dining companion that the titmouse lost his appetite. On the large groaning board outside the kitchen window, Vicki served a banquet of cracked corn and sunflower seeds. Early in March grackles appeared. When a pair landed on the board, they paid less attention to the food than to each other. Both birds hunkered down, pushing themselves into their chests. Then they expanded, necks and breasts swelling, their bills tilting upward, almost lifting them off the feeder. For a moment they swayed toward each other, but then the smaller bird jumped off the board and joined a companionable group of gray squirrels and mourning doves on the ground.

Songs of cardinals rang flowering through early morning. Wanting to see change, I roamed Storrs. People don't so much find what they look for as convince themselves that what they find is what they were looking for. On walks I imagined discovering signs of spring. One morning below the sheep barns a flock of bluebirds foraged through alder and black locust. A familiar sight, the birds spent winter in Storrs, but in March, they now appeared harbingers of another season. Throwing themselves off limbs, the birds seemed to melt like ice along the shore of a pond, sinking blue then rising orange, creating currents that stirred the air into a rich broth of "spring over turn."

As overturn sweeps nutrients up from the bottom of ponds, so spring mixes the high and the low. In spring the goldfinch gets another breast, and the adolescent's fancy turns to lust. Scattered among dry stems of Joe-pye weed near the wolf den were leaves from an issue of *Nugget Extra!* Instead of creating freshness, the new year revived old fleshly delusions. I raked through the table of contents and from the "Fiction" section snagged a tale supposedly written by Daltrey St. James, "Assuming The Throne! Toilet Tart Obsessed With Potty Play!" While the lead article in the "Pictorial" section was "Slave Buys Chinese Mistress The Right Spikes!" the "Fight" department featured "Tit-Tearing Female Fights!" I glanced at a picture. A naked man lay bound to a rack, nineteen clothespins pinching his privates, the ends of the pins sticking up thick as porcupine quills. "Not in these woods," I murmured. "Porcupines don't live in Storrs."

Aside from the magazine I stumbled across few signs of spring. Winds slapped hills, and the metal frame of my glasses burned cold. Near the ski-tow poison ivy clasped the trunks of ashes, rootlets jutting out stiffly, resembling bushy eyebrows. A rough shawl of snow rumpled off the ridge above the Ogushwitz meadow. While boulders tied the hill into knots, fallen trees wrinkled across the slope, snagging line and cable. Without a dress of leaves the forest looked worn and tired. Cankers opened ragged sores, and blisters burst oozing from branches. Lichens pocked bark with age spots, and fungi sloughed off trunks like eczema. Tops of trees dangled down, broken into whisks, and shattered limbs stuck upward in forks. Along the path panes of marbled ice covered depressions while throws of oak leaves buckled through the woods, mottled with damp.

That afternoon I walked the corn fields west of Unnamed Pond. The fragrance of old manure warmed the day. A flock of geese beat low over the woods and planed into a field, air pushing the horseshoes of white feathers on their tails into canters. A turkey scooted across a furrow and vanished between blackberry canes. White-throated sparrows switched whistling through alders. Pokeweed sprawled atop low mounds of rubble, the broken stems dried and white, appearing blasted not by cold but by heat. At the edge of woods paperbark birches bent over, rolling groundward in sweeping curtseys. That night rain and snow stuttered across eastern Connecticut. Early the next morning I drove Eliza to a soccer tournament at the Maybelle B. Avery School in Somers. The sky was doughy, and along the Willimantic River ice clung to the shoreline like pastry to the lip of a pie pan. In Somers gloves of ice grasped scrub, bending limbs into wheels so that bushes seemed to bound through sunlight, tossing blue and yellow sparks into the air.

Foolishness blooms through all seasons. When I returned from Somers, Josh met me in the kitchen. Recently controversy over cloning had spotted newspapers like hives, giving every prattler in the nation vapors. For his part Josh thought cloning might save humanity from the "crepitus bombastus of political mountebanks and the rending nitrosity of night-walking, talon-sharpening spiritual comedians." Precedent for cloning was hallowed. If the Ancient of Days could accomplish it, Josh noted, then chefs in the medical factory should do the same, cloning females, say, from cutlets sliced from males. Once this was accomplished couples would enjoy the same sex drive, and divorce would end. No longer would husbands and wives argue over movies at the video store. Courtship rituals would be simplified. The standard greeting "haven't I seen you somewhere before" would sound absurd and molder away. Because populations would think and act similarly all happenings would be coincidental, and the word *coincidence* would become archaic. Indeed as people embraced the old adage "know thyself," and in a landscape of clones a person could embrace no one other than the self, communication would become intuitive and words themselves would vanish. Because differentiating one self from another would be impossible, discrimination would disappear overnight. The number one song on the Hit Parade would always be "I'm My Own Grandpa." Cloned with the same strengths and weaknesses, people would be truly equal, and democracy would flourish. "Because self-love determines behavior," Josh stated, "peace would spread like measles." Not only armies but governments would disappear. "Paradise would be now and forever." "As generations of me and my rib cage dozed under palms," Josh hymned, "Aurora would swathe our sensibilities with balm. Snakes would sparkle like doves amid a symphony of mosses, and angels would dance through clouds, music trickling tremulous from their wings."

The old gray mare ain't what she used to be, the farmer said to the insurance adjuster, after lightning struck his horse. As months gallop past, doings of days change. Josh, however, remains constant, mocking the platitudinous and reminding people that life isn't simple. "Don't forget," he said at the kitchen door, "the red blackberry is green." The mail is almost as constant as Josh. In March I receive more strange letters than during any other month of the year. Because of weather, people spend a goodly portion of the month in houses. The longer they remain inactive inside, the more they imagine the active and the out-of-doors. As a result they write crank letters. On March 16, I received a letter written on the stationery of the Iowa State Senate. "You have an important letter," the secretary of the English department said when I walked into the office that morning. "The letter is official, and I didn't want to put it in your box and risk losing it," she said, handing me the letter. Printed on the bottom left corner of the envelope and at the top of the stationery itself was a picture of the Iowa Statehouse. Above the building a banner waved. Printed on the banner was "OUR LIBERTIES WE PRIZE AND OUR RIGHTS WE WILL MAINTAIN."

"Dear Professor Pickelring," Ralph Ames, senator from the 31st district began. "Greetings from the State of Iowa on behalf of its citizens. I am writing to invite you to participate in a very special celebration here at the State Capitol April 15, 1997. On that day, the Iowa General Assembly will be holding its annual joint session to honor Iowa citizens who exceed the norm. This year we will honor Mrs. Neoscaleeta Pemberton of The Carts for Wienie Dogs Foundation (TCFWDF) for her fundraising efforts to provide sweatshirts and Billy Bob Halloween costumes for afflicted little dogs of the Wienie breed. In addition and in conjunction with the Iowa Arts Council, we are honoring the Rev. Ephram Zender, President and Founder of the Remain Intact ORGANization (RIO), for his creative efforts in forming the group's motto: 'Circumcision—the unkindest cut of all,' which grew out of his work with the IAC's Mottoes-in-the-Schools program of which our state is justly proud. Because Mrs. Pemberton is also a member of RIO, I understand that this will be the first time in the two-year history of the award that we will so honor an organization twice in a sense. We would like you to address the session and present awards to Mrs. Pemberton and the Rev. Zender, who will receive a plaque and an all-expenses-paid trip to Kansas City to attend a volunteers' conference at the Raphael Hotel. Please be in touch with my assistant for further information. We look forward to hearing your remarks, although I call attention to the attached document and caution you to remember the decorum required by such an event."

The letter was the work of a friend. Each March as snow melts and creeks overflow banks, my friend bounds out of winter, her good humor sweeping high seriousness off its ponderous foundations. Attached to the invitation was a letter written to the senator from Mrs. Pemberton herself on March 10. "Thank you for your letter asking me to recommend someone to speak at the special ceremonies at the Statehouse in April. Through my work with the Foundation, I have been in touch with a Professor Sam Pickelring. Although I do not know him personally, I have made inquiries and believe that—given the proper security arrangements by doorkeepers and guards—he could be allowed to participate on a limited and closely monitored basis. For several years I've been writing to him although I had heard about him for a lot longer (now he says that most of that stuff is not true and was supposed to be expunged from the record after he paid the bribes). As far as I know, he won't steal too much from anyone at the Statehouse, but you should know that I suspect he is a Free Mason. There was that talk a few years ago, but he swears it was all the transsexual's fault."

At this point decorum demands that I skip to the end of Mrs. Pemberton's recommendation. Reputation is fragile, and as readers of my books forever confuse the true with the fabricated, the line between the two being nonexistent, at least in my writings, discretion seems the better clone of cowardice. Be that as it may, Mrs. Pemberton, or Neoscaleeta, as I now address her, concluded her letter to the senator, saying, "I'm looking forward to the gala events at the Statehouse. Rev. Zender and I will meet you at your office at 9:30 if he can get away early from his NoCirc of Iowa Meeting. This may be difficult as the group is having its annual 'Joy of Uncircumcising!' conference with guest speakers discussing restorative procedures."

The next day I received a letter from a Virginian. In February the man had sent me a folk tale. Enclosed in the letter was yet another tale, or "dramatic sunbeam," as he called it. The tale was exuberant, and when composing it, my correspondent, I suspect, suffered from lemon fever, or had been slurping, as blue bloods put it, giggle soup. According to story, however, a tapeworm plagued a prominent Tidewater Republican for a decade. Doctors from all over the South tried to rid the man of the unwanted resident, or squatter, as Democrats inelegantly dubbed the worm. One physician tried to blast the worm out by making the man eat two bushels of black-eyed peas. Instead of swelling bilious, though, the worm thrived. He thought New Year's Eve had arrived, and cramming his head up the man's esophagus, demanded stewed tomatoes. A fisherman from Orvis tied flies shaped like corn on the cob and sweet potatoes and then cast them into the man's stomach. No matter how the fisherman skipped the flies through the bowels, the worm refused to bite. Unfortunately as the fisherman was reeling in a fly shaped like an artichoke, one of the spines speared the man's epiglottis. Extracting the lure was difficult, and the fisherman had to saw through the barb, in the process rupturing a sinus.

Urged by the governor of the state, professors at the Medical College of Virginia sponsored a seminar devoted to separating man from worm. Happily the seminar fashioned a solution. One blistering July day a relay team of physicians chased the man around his house until he began to sweat like a butcher. After he "ran dry," doctors forced the man to lie on his side along the ground. Next the doctors chained the man down then forced him to eat seven country hams. Although the man begged for water, the doctors refused him "even a drop." Near the man's backside the physicians placed a tub brimming with iced tea. Over the man's bottom, the doctors hung a thick rope tied into a hangman's noose. While the man ate ham, the physicians lurked just out of sight behind the curve of his buttocks, all the while, however, studying "the fundament like foxes watching the entrance to the burrow of a groundhog." The ham made the worm thirsty. From the tea fragrances of lemon and sugar wafted cool and so tempting that the worm tossed caution "to the winds" and poked his head out of the man. As soon as the worm's head dipped into the tub, the doctors cinched the rope tightly around his neck then tied the other end of the rope to a Farmall tractor.

Pulling the worm out was difficult and took thirty-eight minutes and fourteen seconds, according to the account published in *The New England Journal of Medicine.* "Forty-two feet long with a neck as thick as a culvert and a mouth resembling that of a snapping turtle, the tapeworm weighed three hundred and ninety-two pounds, twelve ounces." After the worm had been weighed and photographed, the team of doctors standing beside it holding the rope, the manager of a carnival bought the worm and displayed it in an aquarium, claiming it was a monster from twenty thousand leagues under the sea. Although a popular exhibit, the worm proved too expensive for country sideshows, a thirty-seven-and-a-half-pound bag of chicken feed, for example, furnishing only two days of meals.

Eventually an Episcopal minister purchased the worm. Declaring the worm to be a demon he had cast out of the womb of a virgin, the minister made a respectable living exhibiting the creature throughout the church's southern dioceses. Late one Halloween night, however, the worm escaped from a tank at the Tennessee State Fair in Nashville. Hungry, it crawled into the vegetable pavilion where, alas, it choked to death trying to swallow what was billed as "The World's Largest Pumpkin." The following morning a buyer for Brooks Brothers purchased the carcass and shipped it by rail to New York in a refrigerator car. After a boulevardier met the train, a fashion designer oversaw both skinning the worm and tanning the hide. Shortly thereafter Brooks Brothers advertised a line of "Stylish New Alligator Belts." Indirectly the worm also brought wealth to the man who'd acted the part of innkeeper for years. Before the extraction the man was barrelchested. Afterward he was "thin as a grub." Removal of the worm so reduced the man's girth that he received a "mountain of money" for appearing in Before and After advertisements promoting the magical dietary properties of "Dr. Pei Loo's Celestial Stomach Balm and Chinese Fat Extractor."

Like March weather itself my correspondent's letter was a trifle raw. Despite wandering corn fields, I spent much of the month in the library, hunting neither birds nor plants but searching for story, concocting paragraphs describing spring days in Carthage. Rarely does winter chill the pages of my Carthage. The third Saturday in May was workday at the Pillow of Heaven Cemetery. Early that morning families from the Tabernacle of Love gathered in the graveyard. Using shovels, brooms, and hoes, they swept and cut grass from walkways, mounded graves, set fallen stones upright, and planted flowers, starting new beds of periwinkle and setting small pots containing white pansies at the heads of graves. In a low spot far down the slope of Battery Hill, Proverbs Goforth planted a grove of weeping willows. Before lunch much of the conversation was religious. To the surprise of the congregation Orpheus Goforth turned up at ten o'clock. Orpheus knew more about fiddling than about praying. In fact he brought his fiddle and during lunch played "Short'ning Bread." Before lunch he and Loppie Groat mounded graves.

While they worked Loppie catechized Orpheus, asking him, among other things, if he knew where Jesus was buried. The question stumped Orpheus. Still, when Loppie said *Bethlehem*, Orpheus was not at a loss for words. "Shucks," Orpheus said, "I knew He was buried somewhere in Pennsylvania." "I might not know more about theology than a virgin does about dog liver," Orpheus continued, leaning on his shovel. "But I can tell you I'm rowing the fast boat to Glory."

The yellow and blue speckling petals of the pansies made Hoben Donkin ponder heredity. "Do you believe in heredity?" Hoben asked Hink Ruunt as they arranged flowers on the grave of Pony Boguski. "You bet," Hink answered. "I ain't seen it done, but I understand it's an everyday thing in New York City. I'd hate to see it catch on around here, but I wouldn't be surprised if there weren't a couple of cases in Nashville, especially out toward that fancy-pants Belle Meade section." His carnival happening to be performing in Carthage at the time, Hollis Hunnewell helped at the cemetery and drummed up business. Not only did Hollis sell patent medicine and exhibit marvels of nature at the carnival, but he also staged short plays, old favorites such as "Red Hand," "Rip Van Winkle," "Meg Merrilies," and "The Fat Man's Club." Accompanying Hollis to the graveyard was the carnival's lead man, a one-armed actor named Caesar Julius Jelks. Vardis Grawling was more inquisitive than a lawyer, and just being in the company of an actor titillated her. When Vardis saw that Caesar had only one arm, her curiosity practically barked, and she almost dislocated her jaw asking questions. For a while Caesar tolerated the inquisition. But after being turned through two score wrenching questions, he couldn't stand the rack any longer and said, "One final question. I will answer only one more question." "Well, what should it be?" Vardis said coyly, before leaning forward and demanding, "What happened to your arm?" "It was bit off," Caesar said and walked away.

Before he became an actor, Caesar was an inventor. According to Hollis, years earlier Caesar invented a flypaper, one stronger even, he said, than "Steers Chemical Ipecac and Professor Goethe's Matchless Sanative." Unfortunately, as Caesar was hanging a strip of the paper on the clothesline in his back yard, he trod on the opening to a yellow jacket's nest. Hornets swarmed out of the hole. In the rush to avoid being stung, Caesar threw his right arm above his head, in the process slapping it against the flypaper. The paper stuck so tightly to his skin that doctors at Vanderbilt Medical School couldn't pry it loose, and they advised him to seek treatment at the fairgrounds. "A mule team at the state fair might be able to rip it off," the head of the medical school told Caesar. "The prescription was successful," Hollis declared, "but the arm died." The glue held tight. Instead of peeling the paper off, the mules tore out Caesar's arm "fingers and root." "The paper was mighty good," Hollis concluded. After the mule pull Caesar threw the paper and his arm into the trash behind the Homecrafts building. Stuck to the paper the next morning along with the arm, Hollis stated, "were three possums, a prize beagle dog, a bucket of maggots, six bibles, a baby's hand, and four rat tails."

Families brought baskets of food to the workday, and for lunch people ate fried chicken, potato salad, deviled eggs, and fudge cake. Although children and some ladies drank lemonade bought at Barrow's store, most people drank spring water provided by Dapper Tuttlebee. Dapper brought the water in Mason jars, covering the tops with foil to keep flies out. The water was extraordinarily popular, the only complaint coming from Orpheus who reckoned "the water contained a little too much spring." Nevertheless after finishing a jar, Orpheus played the old favorite "The Still House on the Green." During lunch itself Slubey Garts preached a short sermon, urging parishioners to donate to the Sunday school fund, reminding them that shrouds did not have pockets. "He who goes down," Slubey, "never comes up."

The drink made people thoughtful. After lunch the congregation wandered graves and visited old acquaintances. People's minds ran naturally to the element that made the spring water intoxicating, and Turlow Gutheridge told a story about Hiram Povey. When he was young, Hiram dug borax in California. "Did you ever suffer from a burning thirst?" Turlow once asked him in Ankerrow's Café. "Oh, yes," Hiram said. "One time when I was traveling to Barstow, I drank a quart of furniture polish." "Good Lord!" Turlow exclaimed. "Didn't you have any water with you?" "Water?" Hiram said, looking scornful. "What's water got to do with anything? A man suffering from a parched throat doesn't think much about personal cleanliness."

Clevanna Farquarhson strolled over to the grave of Royce, her first husband. When Clevanna started wiping her eyes with a handkerchief, Slubey hurried to her side. "We shouldn't weep," Slubey said. "Royce is only sleeping." "For God's sakes, don't talk so loud," Clevanna whispered. "You might wake the bastard. A passell of son-of-a-bitching spring onions, not grief, caused these here tears." Royce was an unblushing vagabond, so low, Turlow said that "he had to climb a stepladder to get into hell." Still, after lunch the graves of scoundrels attracted more attention that those housing the sanctified. "Flies," Turlow said, "aren't afraid to tickle dead lions." A locksmith by training, Lloyd Griffer used his skills to pick and steal. Even worse, he was a bully. He hated Frank Emberley, for example, who thrashed him after seeing him beat a sick horse. The day after Emberley drowned in an accident at the tannery, Lloyd strolled into the Widow Emberley's yard and with a hoe chopped the head off Sweetkins, little Betsy Emberley's pet kitten. Not long after, Lloyd himself died. One night he tried to steal Davy Crockett, Ben Meadows's Jersey bull. The next morning Ben found Lloyd gored and stomped to death in the pasture, a rope halter twenty yards from the body. The inscription on Lloyd's tombstone was ambivalent, stating, "His Sun Set at Noon. Praise Be to God." "The hanged dog don't bother sheep," Proverbs Goforth said, wrapping his tongue like a slingshot around a wad of tobacco then flinging it hard against the gravestone. "Do you reckon Lloyd's in hell?" Loppie Groat asked. "Is a pig's ass pork?" Proverbs answered. "He's probably enjoying it, though. Buzzards like rotten meat."

Not all after-lunch remarks were critical. After graduating from Carthage High School, Pervis Holland attended Sewanee then the University of Virginia Law School. For years Pervis served on the Federal Court of Appeals in Cincinnati. When he retired, he returned to Carthage and devoted himself to education, serving three terms as head of the Smith County School Board. Some people thought Pervis the most intelligent man in Carthage. According to story when a neighbor sowed nails on Pervis's land, Pervis planted hammers. Next spring when the hammers ripened, they smashed the nails into the ground. On Pervis's death at eighty-six, his wife Lucille had an old-fashioned inscription carved on his stone. "Oh ye young, ye gay, ye proud, / You must die and wear the shroud, / Time will rob you of your bloom, / Death will drag you to your tomb." The verse rankled Carthaginians who thought Pervis deserved a more dignified inscription. "Lucille always had less sense than a Siamese catfish," Turlow said. "Beef at the heels and at the brain," Proverbs added, referring unkindly to Lucille's size. Not surprisingly, shortly after lunch or maybe during dessert, someone etched a new inscription on the back of Pervis's stone. "At This Man's Funeral A Library Was Buried."

When the university closed for spring vacation, students left town. For my part I abandoned books and for nine days roamed Storrs. Years ago when I drifted from organized religion, I hoped that amid Nature I would discover, if not religious truth, at least the stuff of spiritual nourishment. Although impressions of field and wood have made days blossom, I have only stumbled upon common-sensical revelation. Beyond the green wood lurks no deity, and the sky, no matter how domed and cerulean, is not the temple of the numinous. Seeing more in a flower than the flower itself distorts what truths and beauties exist. To know a thing as itself is enough, however. Indeed it is more than people are generally capable of. Forever hoping for, then imposing meaning, people force fiber out of form and so elevate things that life is reduced to a blur. On Palm Sunday I walked for six hours. For a while I regretted the day's having lost religious meaning. But then I realized that the absence of high meaning enabled my walk to be significant, at least significant enough for word and line.

I spent the vacation exploring hills beyond the university's sewerage treatment plant. Once a dump, the land was broken. Moisture seeped out of bruised slopes. Before running into gullies and draining into wetlands, water collected in red pools, chemicals blooming on the surface like pansies. Sweet fern grew brown and scraggly atop mounds of asphalt. Strewn across a trench heaps of sidewalk buckled like the remnants of blasted buildings. A thick pipe jutted out of a pile of gravel, its mouth five inches in diameter and resembling a cannon barrel. A door to a cabinet sank into the ground. Fifty-six inches tall and twenty-three wide, the door made a fine shelter for snakes. In March only a small black cricket lurked underneath. In ample summer snakes would coil like roots, not only beneath the door but throughout the dump, under slabs of plywood, sheets of tar paper, wooden gates, and broken stiles and pallets.

I climbed a brush pile and sat on a stump. While the handle of a shovel leaned against a log, chairs collapsed out of form, rust burning slowly through metal backs and water pulling plugs from wooden seats and legs. Under a board at my feet a ball of caution tape frayed into black and yellow splinters. A grapevine wrapped around a "No Parking" sign, and coils of black hose dried hard and brittle. Near a slab of sidewalk twenty-three blue pipes exploded from a pool of water, resembling a sculpture standing in a giant bird bath. Each pipe was four feet long. Attached to the ends of eleven of the pipes were hunks of concrete shaped like muffins. Amid the concrete, stones shined like hard candy, and the muffins themselves rose, almost as if baking soda had been pumped into them through the pipes. A curved pink lecture table sank into wetlands. If four such tables were placed end to end, they would form a circle. The table was two and a half feet wide, and while the outer edge of the table, the side facing the lecture hall, measured nine feet, three inches, the inner curve, near the lecturer, was five and a half feet long. Reaching the table was difficult. Alders surrounded it, and I picked my way through a lumberyard of scraps, including, among other things, lengths of stairs, from the steps of which boards had fallen into the mud, forming an irregular path.

According to an old Armenian tale Noah was a convivial guy. On the day he finished the ark, Noah visited his closest neighbor. After eating apricots and drinking a pitcher of pomegranate wine, Noah told the man about the flood. "You and your family can join me on the ark," Noah said, "and we'll ride out the high water together." Instead of replying the man scanned the heavens. The sky was gray, and a dark cloud hung over Mt. Ararat, but a seam of light ran so brightly along the eastern horizon that the dark seemed on the verge of lifting like a curtain. "Thanks for the invitation, Brother Noah," the man said. "There is a bit of rain about, but I don't think it will amount to much. I reckon I'll just hunker down here until the sun comes back out."

Occasionally appearances deceive. Much as Noah's neighbor misjudged the weather, so instead of finding the dump inhospitable, life thrived amid the disturbed landscape. On the ridge above the dump a red-tailed hawk perched in a white oak, his tail shuttering like a Venetian blind. A pair of flickers skipped along the edge of the woods while a flock of robins hurried through olives, their movements quick as laughter but their flights low and chortling. While the songs of cardinals sped swift as arrows, those of blue jays bubbled then broke. Beyond the dump a woodpecker thumped a tree, and calls of red-winged blackbirds rose muffled out of wetlands. Crows mobbed a barred owl in the woods, driving him from a maple and harrying him as he blundered above the dump.

As I walked across a hillside, mourning doves clattered into the air. Late one afternoon four buzzards rose over the dump, the long primaries at the tips of their wings scraping the air like fingers digging into water, tilting and ruddering through currents. Under a ridge a fox enlarged the burrow of a groundhog. The fox hunted along the ridge, leaving droppings along the top, usually next to trees. Between a half and three-quarters inches in diameter, the droppings were smaller than those of coyotes. Strings of hair wound through the droppings, and exoskeletons of beetles glistened like slivers of candy. The droppings had fermented, and here and there small white grubs curled contentedly.

Bulldozers having shaved trees from the dump, saplings erupted in bristles, in the damp, alders, female catkins drooping like the feet of ballerinas, rolling above each ankle a thick white sock. Next to the alders rose thickets of gray or field birch, the white bark tinged with green and branches clawing upward out of gray eyes in the bark.

Atop barrows of rubble olive trees grew in webs, the light twigs waving in the light like loose radii. Winter smashed the middles out of many olives, either snapping branches or pinning them to the ground, much as big moths break the hubs of webs.

Brown shafts of mullein stuck out of heaps of gravel. Nearby rosettes of new plants opened along the ground, their leaves resembling wrinkled shammy cloths. Burrs spun around burdock in constellations, spines on the fruits collecting enough of the gray light to glow. Under a rocky chin phragmites grew unkempt and streaked with yellow like an old man's beard. Below an olive a tuft of dandelions bloomed in a bouquet. In wetlands skunk cabbage screwed red and orange upward out of mud. Along the ridge near the fox den boutonnières of wintergreen and rattlesnake plantain clung to the ground, their leaves green and white, exotic against the bare soil. Although March did not bring me face to face with a deity or appoint my days with spirituality, I did see anew. For the first time I noticed horsetails, scouring and variegated scouring rush growing in the damp above the dump, the cone of the latter a bud with a needle tip and the sheath toothed black and white. Such a sight fills the dark sky, as Slubey Garts would put it, "with sweet carolings."

This year Easter ended March. Early Easter Sunday light shone clear and silver. I hid thirty-six eggs in the yard then wandered about until the children woke. A pair of song sparrows scratched the ground under a bird feeder. Atop the feeder perched a brown-headed cowbird, the first of the season. Peonies pushed through the dry grass by the driveway, the tips fat with red. Three crocus bloomed by the woodpile, one yellow and two blue. At the edge of the wood, catkins dangled in tassels from hazelnut. Flower buds on spicebush were swollen, but I saw no sign of bloodroot or dutchman's breeches. Winter had peeled bark from the dead oak by the porch, and locks of grass hung out of an old flicker nest. This year the birds would nest elsewhere. April was in the air as well as on the ground, however, and I knew I would find the nest.

Vicki cooked a leg of lamb for lunch. Before we ate, I read the 114th Psalm, the Easter Psalm. "The mountains," David declared, "skipped like rams, and the little hills like lambs." When I read "which turned the rock into a standing water, the flint into a fountain of waters," Eliza said, "that's spring." The following afternoon snow started falling. The next morning was the first of April. At seven o'clock sixteen inches of snow were on the ground, and I trudged around the yard. Two downy woodpeckers squawked in the woods, and doves huddled on branches like students waiting for a lecture to begin. Palms of snow pressed the yews flat, but I noticed that cornelian cherries were blooming. Each year soon after the cherries bloom, spicebush blossoms, and colors riot through days. I pushed through a drift, and snow reached my thigh. The world was quiet, the sort of place that transforms tongues into pens. Suddenly I wanted to scroll days back to the beginning of March, "that reassuring stable month," as Eliza described it.

An Orgy of Southernness

*I*n April I attended the Festival of Southern Autobiography in Conway, Arkansas. In Storrs snow still bulged out of curbs, and seams of fibrous ice stretched taunt as forearms through woods. In Conway daffodils, crepe myrtle, and pink and white dogwood blossomed soft and sudsy, scrubbing winter out of yards and minds. Participants in the festival stayed at the local Ramada Inn. The day we arrived was sunny, and after dropping a bag in his room, a novelist who lives in Philadelphia jumped into a bathing suit, raced outside, and dove into the motel pool. At four o'clock the next morning the novelist was awakened by his right ear throbbing like an alarm clock. Before breakfast he bought a bottle of rubbing alcohol and throughout the day tossed shot glasses of "juice" down his ear. "Not knowing Conway was dry, I bought the booze to drink," he explained, adding that when he learned buying liquor was illegal he dumped the alcohol down his ear in hopes that a few heeltaps would seep through the eardrum then trickle down his throat.

That afternoon the novelist examined the pool closely. A rug of fungus rumpled over the bottom. The excitement of spring having temporarily blinded him, he hadn't noticed the fungus before. Amid the seaweed he discovered two dead Siamese cats, a bulldog, fourteen hamsters, and a midget. The midget had been submerged so long that decay had untied his joints and stretched his limbs so that he was seven feet, six inches tall. As a result, the novelist recounted, all the leading basketball schools in the country were trying to recruit him. In the restaurant at the Ramada Inn, the novelist said he had met coaches from Arizona State, the University of Nevada at Las Vegas, Princeton, Cincinnati, Stanford, Long Beach, Kansas, and Michigan. Because the midget was not lively, he was, in the vernacular of athletics, "a project." Still, because he was quiet, he was not likely to prove an academic embarrassment during post-game interviews. Moreover, the NCAA had declared the midget eligible to play immediately, the disability of death having exempted him from the Scholastic Aptitude Test.

"An orgy of southernness," a short story writer said after the novelist described the midget. "Stories bloom rank throughout the day." Atop a table in the motel lobby perched a bowl filled with religious tracts, all published in Fort Worth by "Sowers Of Seed." Earlier that morning the novelist had stuffed a batch of tracts into his pocket. Instead of answering the short story writer, the novelist handed him a tract entitled *Let Not Your Heart Be Troubled*, the heart appearing not as a word on the title page but as a bloody lump. Printed on the back cover of the tract was an excerpt from Proverbs. Before giving the short story writer the tract, the novelist circled the excerpt, drawing a blue line around it with a gold ball-point pen: "A Merry Heart Doeth Good Like A Medicine: But A Broken Spirit Drieth The Bones."

Southerners do two things well, a poet told me. "They tell stories, and they argue over who comes from the poorest background, trying to one-down, not one-up, each other, saying things like, 'At least your grandfather's house was painted. My grandfather's house wasn't painted and didn't have a porch, not even a stoop'." "Of course," the poet continued, "that last statement is the beginning of a tale. Before the teller finishes the story, the house will have a tar paper roof, a tin pipe chimney, and window panes cut from a roll of wax paper."

Participants in the festival lived lives as structured as formal gardens, their days terraced and their behaviors as regular as yews clipped into geometry. Only their words grew weedy. Not whacked out of life by platitude, the words attracted bees, butterflies, and paragraphs. In Connecticut I spend days in libraries, beating through books in hopes of flushing stories. In Arkansas stories rose clattering from conversation. A woman told me that the skin of "one of her lovers smelled like fresh rain on red clay." Conway was in the middle of "Tornado Alley," and tornado shelters resembling humped underground garages had been built in many yards. At the urging of a novelist, a professor at the University of Central Arkansas drove participants in the festival around Conway, pointing out shelters. "Whenever I see a tornado shelter," the novelist said, "I just can't help myself."

One night I watched high school seniors getting into limousines in order to attend a dance. "Look at the figures on those girls," a storyteller said, strolling up behind me. "When I was fifteen I only had one tit, and I didn't get another until I was twenty-three and pregnant." The students had eaten dinner in a posh restaurant. Two women left the restaurant just after the students. "Was it fun being around those kids?" I asked. "And how!" one of the women answered. "Anne Howe?" The storyteller said immediately. "Do you know her? She's my cousin, and her husband is a good friend of the governor." For a moment the women looked puzzled, then one spoke, saying, "I'm afraid we don't know her. We're not from around here. We're from Texas and are on our way to see our nephew in Memphis." "Texas? That doesn't make any difference," the storyteller said. "Anne Howe's husband shoots dove with the Governor of Texas, and I have heard, but don't breathe a word of this to anybody, that he steps out with the Governor of Tennessee."

Habit accompanies a person on his travels. Although I studied the pool at the Ramada Inn, I did not see the midget, though as my eyes stirred through the fungus, I did find the bulldog, one of the cats, not Siamese but Persian, however, and at least six of the hamsters, the fur covering two of them violet, though, not brown. Those observations aside, however, in Connecticut I spend more time in wood and field than I do in conversation. Instead of jotting down parts of speech, I describe parts of plants, pistils and stigmas rather than nouns and verbs. Writers spent the last night of the festival at the Capital Hotel in Little Rock. Lilies bloomed at the entrance to the hotel, twelve pots circling the lip of a round table, the flowers white trumpets celebrating spring. Ferns hung in fans over the lilies while brushes of bromeliads jutted through fronds, looking as if they had been dipped into pink butter. Once I saw the flowers, season, rather than spicy conversation, appealed to me, and after checking into my room, I left the hotel and wandered the banks of the Arkansas River.

In the sun the brown river shone like leather. The current pushed

Styrofoam cups into coves where they snagged on roots then swished back and forth, from a distance resembling broken seed pods. Two men fished from a floating dock lashed to the shore, one man sitting on a crate, the other on an inverted trash can. Pigeons bustled beneath bridges, their wings busy as pencils. Robins hunted worms along the embankment, and mockingbirds hurried about, their tails flashing like semaphores. A kingbird perched on a branch, her body immobile but her head occasionally ticking as she searched for insects. Viceroy butterflies slid low over grass, bouncing across invisible moguls. In the brush above the river, leaves from cottonwood trees slumped together in gray heaps, the seedpods of honey locust twisting through them like black tape. Leaves on black cherries had just unfolded, and seining silver out of the sunshine glistened watery. While blossoms on princess trees crinkled like purple tissue paper, smooth seams curled through the bark, resembling ripples of light.

I stopped at the Riverfront Belvedere and listened to a young man playing an electric guitar and singing country music. I didn't recognize the songs, but I noticed that he wore a straw cowboy hat through the crown of which six air holes had been punched. Exactly at one o'clock the man stopped singing and walked to a picnic table where he ate lunch with his wife and small baby, and two older people who appeared to be his wife's parents. The singer played with the child, strumming his toes like guitar strings. I wondered if the man was from Little Rock, and if he were paid. Maybe, I thought, he sings in hope of attracting the attention of someone who will cart him to Nashville and golden fame.

Suddenly trees and birds no longer interested me, and I walked up from the river into the town, looking for threads of story. Almost immediately I noticed details of place and mood. A ragged dog limped along Second Street, a mockingbird swooping above him scolding, occasionally dropping out of the air and pecking him atop the head. Taped to the window of Mr. Cool, a store located at 301 Main Street, was a square of yellow paper. Printed in black on the paper was "14K GOLD TOOTH CAP $12.99." I crossed the street and entered Bennett's Military Supplies. In display cases eviscerators lay as close as teeth, all of them steel-capped and manufactured in Pakistan. A "Lipstick Knife" cost $4.95. When the top was pulled off the case, a blade big enough to castrate a bull sprang up. While I was in Bennett's, a man wearing green trousers bought a black T-shirt. The man's hair was dyed yellow, and tattoos scrolled over his arms and neck like ornaments decorating the backs of playing cards. When I left Bennett's, I studied the store's window displays. In the front window a heavy machine gun pointed skyward. Pasted around the edges of all the windows was the electric tape of a burglar alarm. Behind glass panes but stretching across the bottom of each window like sharp picket fences were cactus. Tall and prickly, the fence may have deterred thieves more than the alarm. I recognized several varieties of cactus: white tower, blue flame, organ-pipe and toothpick, the spines of this last white splinters tipped with black.

In Connecticut slipping from sight is easy. Crossing a ridge or drifting off a path erases my presence. Disappearing from storyland is more difficult. Sunday morning at the airport the man behind the TWA counter checked my ticket then said, "You must be a Democrat." That night at dinner I asked Vicki if I looked like a Democrat. "No," she said. "You don't look like much of anything. Why?" After I described the encounter at the check-in, Vicki asked if the clerk was southern. "Yes," I answered, "but what does that have to do with anything?" "Well," she said getting up from the kitchen table and walking over to the sink, "that simply explains that."

A telephone call interrupted the conversation. Dick Ottarson had just died in Nashville. For sixty-one years Dick was married to my cousin Kathryn Pickering, and I had known and loved Kathryn and Dick before I had affections. On Tuesday I flew from Providence to Nashville. I stayed that night with Bill Weaver, my oldest friend. After dinner Bill showed me sketches of the house he and Nicky, his wife, planned to build on a bluff at Monteagle, six miles from our undergraduate school Sewanee. Bill is a successful businessman, and during the conversation his business acumen shined on me and made story bud. Bill's house stood on a blue spur of the Cumberland Plateau. Two thousand feet below, a green valley opened like a hand, creeks and fences running across it like lines indenting a palm. "Land under the mountain isn't expensive," I said to Bill. "I am going to buy three acres from the farmer who owns the valley and build a galoshes factory. The first thing I'll erect will be a billboard advertising 'Pickering's Rubbers'. Every morning when you eat breakfast on the deck, you will see the sign and remember your old buddy Sam. Like the good friend I am I will be doing you a favor, too. Never will you go out of the house on a rainy day without overshoes." "Of course," I continued, "if you don't think you need to be reminded about rainwear, you can buy the land from me for, say, the neighborly price of a million dollars an acre." Before getting into my pajamas, I told Bill that I wouldn't start building the factory until after the foundation of his house had been laid, explaining that I didn't want him to feel pressured into purchasing my holdings. "I will instruct the farmer to raise hogs on the land," I said. "Once the concrete in your foundation is hard, however, the pigs become hams and the sign goes up."

Early the next morning I visited Montgomery Bell Academy, a country day school in Nashville. I attended high school at MBA and after college taught English there for a year. Two years ago I was appointed to the school's Board of Advisors, the appointment being, I thought at the time, an effort to add financial diversity to the Board, all the other members being moneyed. Now as I drove to MBA, I was no longer certain that sociological concern motivated the appointment. Perhaps, I thought, members of the Board knew me better than I knew myself and guessed that one bright dawn I would flash across their days like a broker, golden dealings having transformed me from a teacher into "The Rubber King."

I roamed the grounds at MBA, looking for a trace of an earlier self. Although exteriors of buildings appeared the same as when I attended the school, interiors had been gutted. In contrast, time had gutted or trenched my exterior while my interior or at least my mind had remained childish. As I strolled though the Ball Building discussing educational method with the headmaster, my thoughts tumbled back over the years. The gap between word and thought is vast and in the middle of a paragraph on teaching poetry, I stuffed a pickle into Lionel Barrett's left ear. While quoting Tennyson's "Ulysses," my tongue measuring each step carefully, my mind galloped around the Carter Building, Lionel a stride behind, a wad of ballpark mustard in his right hand.

I moved to New England thirty years ago. In Connecticut I don't have a past or a youth to visit. My past lives in Tennessee, and whenever I visit the south, I remember beginnings and imagine endings. Remarks are significant in the south because they immediately become parts of narratives, both stories and lives. In New England, remarks are dissociated from story and are significant only in themselves, becoming the stuff of intellectual not communal play. The same holds true for things. In the south, instead of simply furnishing rooms, things are associated with lives and become the appointments of story.

In New England, however, I am freer that I am in the south. Hours are my own, and instead of pulling me to people, my wanderings take me nowhere. From MBA I hurried off to visit friends of my parents, five people who like Dick Ottarson were in their eighties. Later in the day I ate lunch at Vandyland. I have eaten at Vandyland for fifty years, starting when Vandyland was named Candyland and Mother and Father and I lived in the Sulgrave Apartments. I sat at the counter, on the same stool on which I sat seven years ago when I was last in Nashville. I ordered my usual lunch: a double chocolate soda and a chicken salad sandwich on toast. After eating I drove to West End Methodist Church. The funeral did not begin for two hours, so I walked across the street to Vanderbilt to see how many of my essay collections were in the bookstore. Almost never do I find my books in stores, but at Vanderbilt, I found three.

I knew all the people attending the funeral. Even when I could not identify faces, I recognized names and attached them to histories. The flowers on the altar were also familiar: roses, dogwood, purple lilac, branches of fresh crabapple, and pink trumpet lilies. The two hymns sung were old favorites, and I sang the first two stanzas of "Amazing Grace" and the first four of "O God, Our Help in Ages Past" without opening the hymnal. "A thousand ages in thy sight / Are like an evening gone; / Short as the watch that ends the night / Before the rising sun," declared the fourth stanza of "O God." The time I had been away from Nashville suddenly resembled an evening gone. I had lived paragraphs elsewhere, but now those sentences seemed only expansions of what occurred earlier on my page. Certainly I did not write new topic sentences after I left Tennessee; the old ones were hardy perennials and still described mood and thought accurately. At the end of the service I walked with Kathryn back to the vestry. After I sat for a short time, she told me to go. Twice I left the room then returned to hug her, grasping not simply someone I loved but memory itself, holding her tightly in hopes that recollection would not shift shape and blur.

Late that afternoon I drove to Sewanee, memory, not spring, greening the hills. Along the road redbuds glowed like clouds at sunset, and dogwood blossoms fell through cedars in showers. As Bill Weaver is godfather to my first son Francis, George Core, editor of the *Sewanee Review*, is godfather of Edward, my second boy. George booked me into Rebel's Rest, the guesthouse at Sewanee, and that night he and Susan, his wife, took me to dinner. After dinner George and I talked about books and friends. That night recollection whirred through my head, and I had trouble sleeping. A bookcase leaned against the wall in the dining room at Rebel's Rest. Most volumes in the case were yearbooks, two of them from my student years at Sewanee. I did not read the yearbooks, however. Instead I took a mystery from the case, E. Phillips Oppenheim's *The Last Ambassador or, the Search for the Missing Delora*. Before I fell asleep, I read 158 pages. The next morning I stuffed the book into a bag and took it to the airport with me so that I would have something to read on the plane. "You stole this book," Vicki said when I unpacked. "No, I didn't steal it," I said. "Well, then, what do you call it?" Vicki asked. "I don't know," I said. "But I didn't steal it. I don't steal books."

Vicki said more about the *Missing Delora*, but I didn't listen. I was thinking about something that happened at the airport in Nashville. The flight to Providence left from gate seven in terminal C. In the waiting area I noticed a woman my age standing beside the counter. She attracted me, and before I realized it, I was only a yard away from her. "Good golly, this is odd," I thought. I'm not a masher, so I turned quickly and walked back along the corridor to a café and bought a cup of coffee. I hoped the woman would be gone when I returned to the waiting area. She was still there, sitting in a chair staring at people strolling through the terminal. I put my bag down, and taking out the *Delora*, sat in a chair near her. I did not read, however. I also watched people. After a large girl wearing a pink shirt strolled past chewing a fist of bubble gum, I leaned toward the woman sitting in the chair and said, "You have really been watching folks. Have you seen anything interesting?" The woman turned my way, stared, then said, "Don't I know you?"

I attended Vanderbilt for a year. One of the reasons I transferred to Sewanee was that coeducation made me uncomfortable. At Vanderbilt a girl named Cornelia was in most of my classes. Cornelia had brown hair and a bright smile, and when she was in a room, I could not concentrate on books. I never asked her for a date because I was seventeen and dreamed of seeing "the world." I suspected that if I went out with her once I would eventually marry her. After I transferred to Sewanee, I dreamed, not of high seas and faraway places, but of Cornelia.

Only after we introduced ourselves did I recognize Cornelia. "When I was a freshman, I had such a crush on you," she said. "I had a crush on you, too," I said. "Forty years have passed, and I still think you are super," I said, whereupon people sitting close to us burst into applause. Cornelia and I chatted like the old friends we had almost been. She married just after college and had three children. She was at the airport to meet two grandchildren flying to Nashville from New Orleans. I told her about my family, and redbud and dogwood seemed to bloom in the airport. Soon my flight was called. Before I left, Cornelia introduced me to her granddaughters. That night I described the meeting to an acquaintance in Connecticut. "You should have raced off to a motel and tumbled amorously against each other in a big bed," he said. "That would have brought the story to a smashing conclusion." "No," I said. "That's a northern, not a southern ending." "Real endings are beginnings," I explained. After meeting the girls, I got Cornelia's address. I told her that I wanted my boys to marry warm, good-natured girls. "When the time comes for the boys to fall in love," I said, "I'm going to mail them to you and your granddaughters in Tennessee." "That will never happen," my friend said. "Yes, it will," I said. "On paper the story will end just that way. I will shape the pages of the boys' lives so that they don't run away from happiness."

Two days later I received a letter from Bill Weaver. He said that he would help me market my galoshes "for a price." Then he said that he and Nicky enjoyed my visit. "It was fun to invigorate our friendship,"

he wrote, adding "what are good friends for?" However, he continued, "we had your bedroom hosed down and fumigated as we found
some head lice on the pillow. We also put ammonia on the walls in
the bedroom. Actually we found head lice in the office and the new
room and every place you had been. We had to have the whole house
hosed down with ammonia and fumigated. The problems did not end
there because the lice migrated to my neighbor's house, and we also
had to fumigate and hose down his house with ammonia. It cost me
$10,000, but what are old friends for? We look forward to your next
visit, but give us a little time to recover from the expense of this last
visit." I read the letter to Vicki. "You don't have nits," Vicki said.
"Somebody else must have left bugs in the room." "No, Bill's letter is
the beginning of a story," I said, "a funny story." "Funny?" Vicki said.
"I don't get it."

Deprived of Unhappiness

"*I* want you to write a memoir," the agent wrote. "Autobiography sells." Eliza agreed with the agent. "Write one of those whiny self-help books," she said. "Pitiful people love them." Habit runs bone deep. Much as the youthful me never pretended to be sensitive, not even when a doleful countenance could win affection, so now I couldn't feign unhappiness for money. Since my parents were wonderful, responsible people, since I had not suffered through a sexual identity crisis, since I was never chosen last for a schoolyard team and was voted "Most Popular" my senior year in high school, since eating disorders, alcoholism, and incest did not make my childhood endlessly fascinating, I was afraid, I wrote the agent, that my autobiography would have to be entitled *Deprived of Unhappiness*, "not a phrase likely to inspire sappy, sales-boosting publicity."

The agent did not answer the letter. The successful memoir is almost always inspirational. Either born in or damned to suffering, the hero displays admirable resilience and through a combination of pluck and good humor overcomes adversity, in the process being transformed from, as Josh put it, a hopeless case into a role model, "concern for others and a bank account clotting veins and curdling prose." Much as memoirs predictably ascend from the gritty to the ethereal, so people think platitudinously. The day after I wrote the agent a teacher assigned Eliza a research paper. "You can write about anything," the teacher said, "so long as you describe a tragedy followed by a triumph." "Daddy, I want to write about the Armenian massacre in Turkey," Eliza said that night, "but how could there be a triumph if hundreds of thousands of people were slaughtered? I asked the teacher, and she said that maybe someone learned a lesson and became better." "There was no triumph, only horror and damnation," I said. "No lesson was learned. Man never learns from the past. If a historian ever tells you that we study history so that we will not repeat the mistakes of the past, you are talking to a dreamer, a person so bent on observing a butterfly metamorphosing within the silk of tragedy that he refuses to see that parasites have drained life from the caterpillar and reduced the cocoon to a shell."

Hard history aside, what makes one person happy often doesn't affect another. "You can't expect people to see things alike," Turlow Gutheridge said last week to Loppie Groat. "Of course you can't," Loppie answered. "Why, different folks don't even look alike." For my part I'm satisfied with simple things. Never do I jump under a low ceiling, and the modest runs of my books do not chafe me into irritability. In my world sentence is strong enough to shred gray mood into wisps. "That's the pot calling the kettle beige," a man said recently in the Cup of Sun, making me smile. Thursday I started reading *What's Happened to the Humanities*. On coming into the bedroom to wish me good-night, Edward saw the book. "Humanities?" he said. "Aren't they those fat porpoises that live in Florida?" Yesterday a neighbor brought three copies of my latest book, *The Blue Caterpillar*, by the house for me to sign. When she could not find the book in the university store, the neighbor told a clerk. The clerk immediately telephoned the storeroom and said, "Can you send up some caterpillars from the basement?"

My essays spin slowly through paragraphs. Occasionally I pretend to accelerate or at least to keep abreast of swift fashionable doings. In truth, however, I resemble the snail who after dragging himself onto the fender of a junked car shouted, "Floor it. I'm in a hurry." Like the car the stories I tell are stationary. The narratives don't teach or inspire. Readers know my hankerings and often send me stories, not tales plucked fluttering from the air but dozy comfortable caterpillars who enjoy basement life. In May I received two stories, both placed in Carthage, Tennessee, and both describing the antics of my characters.

"Last month a pack peddler wandered through town selling alligator bags," a man wrote. The peddler claimed he'd killed then skinned the alligators and made the bags himself. He tried to sell the Widow

Warple a battered purse resembling a football, one, my correspondent said, "which looked like a relic from the Vanderbilt-Tennessee game." "This bag is awfully scuffed," the widow said, rubbing her right hand across the purse. "All gator bags are rough," the drummer responded. "Roughness is a sign of being genuine. After a hunter shoots an alligator out of a tree, the skin gets scuffed when the creature falls through the branches to the ground." "Some time back," another correspondent wrote, "Googoo Hooberry and Hoben Donkin rented a boat and went fishing on Center Hill Lake." After pulling in a string of largemouth bass, Googoo turned to Hoben and said, "This is the best fishing hole I've ever seen. Your eyesight is better than mine. Mark the spot so we can come here again." Later as Googoo was tying the boat up at the dock, he asked Hoben if he marked the place. "Yes, indeed," Hoben said, "I scratched a cross on the side of the boat just over the fishing hole." "You ignoramus!" Googoo exclaimed, throwing his rod on the dock in exasperation, "how do you know we'll get this boat the next time we go fishing?"

Some readers lack the capacity to appreciate such stories, particularly readers nurtured on literary diets heavy with spiritual or intellectual uplift. Recently a New Yorker wrote me, saying that although he found the beginnings of my essays intriguing he just couldn't push through "all that country twaddle." Unlike tragedy and triumph, twaddle makes me happy. When I received the letter, I had not written twaddle in some time. After putting the man's letter down on my desk, I picked up my pencil and was soon deep in the country. During the time I neglected to write twaddle Hollis Hunnewell brought his carnival back to Carthage.

A new aquarium increased attendance. The aquarium resembled a baptismal font with a glass front, the kind of font popular in sophisticated Baptist churches. Schools of perch, crappie, long green eels, and large- and smallmouth bass splashed through the aquarium. A fat snapping turtle hunkered down in the middle of a whitewalled tire at the bottom of the aquarium, the turtle's shell resembling a battered hubcap, its beak sticking up like a hard inner tube. Pasted to the front of the aquarium along the bottom were scallop shells painted different colors: red, green, blue, and orange. While a stuffed pelican perched on the upper left corner of the aquarium, an alligator basked on the right, a light bulb screwed in its mouth. The main attraction of the aquarium, however, was the "Man Fish." On electric poles throughout Smith County Hollis nailed signs reading "Amazing Man Fish" and "The Aquatic Wonder Born to a Chinese Mermaid in the Yangdoodle River." Across the back of the aquarium stretched a plaster of Paris rock with a flat surface. The man fish lounged atop the rock, resting on a mound of pillows, all covered with chintz, the fabric blooming with shells and fish, rather than the usual fruit and flowers.

The man fish did not talk although occasionally it raised its left arm, and Hollis handed it a cigarette. From the waist down the man fish resembled a dime-store mermaid, green scales the size of dessert plates covering what on a normal person would have been legs. While a pink fin as large as two church fans waved at the end of the man fish's body, a fuzz of hair resembling a crew cut covered the creature's head. A thick black mustache hung over the fish's upper lip. Jutting out from the beneath the fish's ears and running around and behind its neck was a white gill, stiff and pleated like a ruffle. With the exception of head and neck, though, the man fish resembled a woman from the waist up. The creature's bosom was large and pendulous, and when the animal shifted on the pillows, its breast tumbled, rolling against its chest like cantaloupes shaking in a bushel basket. Aside from dairy farmers and reprobates who had visited Adam and Eve clubs in Nashville, most Carthaginians had never seen such impressive "lactaters," as Turlow Gutheridge described them.

After studying the aquarium, Quintus Tyler, senior teacher at the Male and Female Select School, urged Sheriff Baugham to close the carnival, saying the creature looked "ready to spawn" and was guilty of indecent exposure. "Shut down the carnival!" the sheriff exclaimed. "Quintus, you are a teacher. Can't you read? The sign says 'Man Fish.' When men swim in the Cumberland River, they take off their shirts. So long as a man covers his pringle, he can't be arrested for indecent exposure. I've spent considerable time looking at the fish, and I haven't seen even a hint of a pringle. A fellow doesn't get a chance to see this sort of thing very often," the sheriff concluded, adding that "if I was you, Quintus, I'd declare a holiday so all the boys could go to the carnival."

"How is your writing going?" Eliza said, walking into the study just as I polished the scales on the man fish. "Swimmingly," I said. It was time to drive Eliza to soccer practice in Ashford. Spitting out the hook of twaddle is not easy. This spring I wrote Slubey Garts and asked why there were no mirrors in the Haskins Funeral Home. Proverbs Goforth answered the letter on Slubey's behalf. I read Proverbs's reply while Eliza scurried about the soccer field. Consideration for the deceased led Slubey to remove the mirrors, Proverbs explained. "No matter what paints and creams undertakers slather on dead folks," Proverbs wrote, "corpses don't look lively." "If a dead person glances in a mirror, chances are he ain't going to like what he sees. A dead person needs to feel good about himself when he lines up at the box office outside the Pearly Gates. Appearance matters, and if a corpse believes he looks his best, he'll ooze confidence, and St. Peter will probably hand him a ticket without asking him a question, not even his Social Security number."

According to Bavarian story, God created Adam with seven tongues. Not only did the tongues get in the way of each other, often making Adam tongue-tied, but because each tongue spoke a different language confusion entered the world and accompanied Adam's descendants around the globe. Eventually six of the tongues withered and disappeared. In contrast, the languages not only multiplied but also grew so complex that a babble of interpretation now undermines happiness. In my essays sentences are short. Instead of interpreting, and confusing, I describe. In the attic recently I found a hundred-year-old advertisement for Sunlight Soap. Measuring five by three and a half inches, the advertisement resembled a seed packet. "Woman," the back of the packet stated, "stood for hours over the steaming odors of poisonous materials and inhaled bad health. SUNLIGHT SOAP *altered all that.* It did away with the toil which *shattered the life of the housewife."* Covered with gray, stenciled paper, the front of the packet looked like a parlor wall. On the wall hung a gold frame. In the middle of the frame a woman wearing a red dress and a filthy cotton fichu around her neck bent over a washtub. While perspiration rolled off the woman's forehead, she held a thick scrub brush in her right hand. In her left hand she clutched a stained cloth, her fingers arthritic and as wrinkled as the cloth. On a table behind the woman a candle burned to a nub, the scene implying that woman had scrubbed clothes all day.

Printed in white letters along the side of the washtub was the phrase "The Old Way."

A tab jutted out from the bottom of the packet. When the tab was pulled, the picture in the frame changed. Now the woman sat before a window reading a magazine, her dress pressed and the fichu smooth and white. Outside the window washing danced on a clothesline. On the wall to the right of the woman's head hung a clock, the time five before one in the afternoon, illustrating that when housewives used "The Sunlight Way" woman's work ended before lunch.

As pulling the tab changed the woman's life, so noticing small things makes my days dance. Yesterday I saw three young groundhogs, not one of them bigger than a fist. When I sat down within a yard of them, the smallest growled. After a moment, though, the groundhog ignored me and returned to cropping grass with his litter mates. I spent much of yesterday ferrying children across town, taking Eliza to Dr. Dardick then after an early dinner driving Edward to a baseball game in Windham Center. Rain fell throughout the game, and I returned home cold and weary. As I stepped into the kitchen, however, I noticed a moth clinging to the screen door. A sliver of brown velvet lined with white, the moth was a Baltimore Bomolacha, a species I had not seen before. Suddenly the air dried; cold vanished, and I felt energetic and content.

The very notion of a triumph turns me cowardly or, as Loppie Groat phrased it, "feather-legged." Dreaming of success will eventually sour a man's Adam's apple, as high expectations are rarely fulfilled. A person can want something so long that eventually it loses its appeal. Indeed achieving a dream deferred often brings resentment, not gratification. As moths on screens flicker upon my inward eye brighter than comets, so I have grown accustomed to the sales of my books. If a collection of my essays were to become a best-seller, I would be irritated and fearful. Success would disrupt the quiet tenor of life, making the possession of extraordinary goods possible. Success also might tempt me with the bads, peeling the marvelous from the ordinary and so distorting judgment that I might think that I had been deprived of happiness for decades.

In part happiness depends upon exorcising the expectation of superlatives from daily living. Vicki and I have been married a round of years. On the first nine the going was easy. As the children have grown into importuning, though, the back nine has been difficult. Indeed after a decade bogies become pars for married couples. Recently the rough has become higher. Boundaries have shrunk, and Vicki no longer allows free drops. Nowadays I stumble into hazards unimagined when I teed up on the first hole. My irons have melted. Sand traps swallow my chip shots, and I wobble when I putt. Because I expected my handicap to soar, however, strolling the years with Vicki has been fun. Days remain green, and occasionally Vicki pauses in the shade beside a fairway and, tossing Izod sweaters and knickers into the golf bag, shreds the scorecard and declares the time has come for "a sweat shirt and socks jamboree," a phrase that middle-aged men-and-women fish understand.

In a good life things don't turn up. Instead they are turned up. Rummaging through the everyday keeps me content. Francis is a sophomore in high school. This fall he took the Preliminary Scholastic Aptitude Test. He did well, and although he will not graduate from high school for two more years, letters from colleges have almost burst the mailbox. One day he received sixteen letters from, among others, Clemson, New York University, Emory, Manhattanville, Denison, Sacred Heart, the University of Miami, Richmond, LaSalle, Boston University, and the Marine Corps, this last promising a "Marine Corps Key Lanyard" if he returned a card requesting a copy of the Corps' *Opportunity Book.* "Dear Francis," the letter from the University of Chicago began, "Your scores on the PSAT suggest that you look forward to surrounding yourself with fellow students and teachers who care deeply about books, ideas, art, dialogue, community, and life. If so, you should know more about the University of Chicago." "We have just received word of your excellent performance on the PSAT," the director of admissions at Cornell declared. "Given your scores and your fine achievement in school, I am confident you would thrive on the intellectual challenges of a great school such as Cornell." The University of Southern California advertised a Resident Honors Program that enabled "successful students like you to complete their high school requirements while enrolled as full-time freshmen. As an RHP student, you will receive a significant merit scholarship and you may also be eligible for need-based financial aid. You'll have access to the faculty and facilities of one of America's largest private research universities, while living in a small community with other exceptional students."

Francis rowed for E. O. Smith High School this spring. Because he rarely got home before six-thirty in the evening, he did not read the letters. Always ready to catch a crab, whether in a boat or out, I read every letter. St. John's College in Maryland sent a list of "Great Books" students read. During their freshman year students read books by Homer, Aeschylus, Sophocles, Thucydides, Euripides, Herodotus, Aristophanes, Plato, Aristotle, Euclid, Lucretius, Plutarch, Nicomachus, Lavoisier, and Marcus Aurelius. Thirty-five years ago I read to dawn, night after night studying authors on a similar list in hopes, as Francis Bacon put it, of becoming "a full man." I read so much that I burst. Nowadays I read temperately, dining on a literary cuisine light with essays and mysteries. More to my mature taste than the St. John's regimen was a list of "Summer Reading Suggestions From The Kenyon College Faculty." Twenty-six volumes comprised the list, one book of poetry, eleven novels, and fourteen works of nonfiction. I had read many of the books. Some, however, I had long meant to read, and the next morning I bought three volumes at the university store: Michael Malone's novel *Handling Sin*, E. O. Wilson's autobiography *Naturalist*, and Tobias Wolff's memoir *This Boy's Life*.

A card and a brochure usually accompanied each letter. Schools instructed interested students to return the cards after listing their academic and extracurricular activities. Except for the card sent by Oberlin College the cards were similar. Printed on the card from Oberlin was an "optional question": "How do you describe yourself?" Francis could select from seven options: "Hispanic, Latino," "Asian / Pacific Islander," "White," "Eskimo, Aleut," "Native American," "Black / African American," "Multiracial (specify)," or "Other (specify)." Francis does not yet think of himself in racial terms. He is a tall, red-headed boy who rows and makes good grades and who has a lot of sweet, kooky friends. He won't drink soda or eat hamburgers. One day last month forty-seven hundred people visited his homepage, and he received one hundred and nineteen e-mails, all of which he deleted unread. He is his daddy's lovely boy, not some variety of "specify." I dropped the card from Oberlin into the garbage can.

In brochures colleges appeared bucolic places, and for a moment I longed to be seventeen again. Dabs of blue water spotted Carleton's green Arboretum. Ionic columns transformed Allegheny's Brooks Hall into a Greek temple. At Georgia Tech a green lawn rolled out from a French Romanesque Revival building then unspooled into ribbons of red and yellow tulips. While color slipped from behind the tracery of Gothic windows into a dining hall at Kenyon, at Reed live oaks spooned light from the air, dappling the ground below. At Cornell two students pushed bicycles across an arching stone bridge. Below the bridge, water slouched across mossy ledges before rippling and sliding electric over a rocky fall.

The year imposes rhythms upon life. In spring activities so clutter days that I rarely pause for introspection, much less ponder happiness. Examinations begin in early May. This year a student broke his hand the day before the exam, and I quizzed him orally. Another student ran a high fever, and I wrote a separate exam for her and let her take it in my office. Three students showed up at the wrong time, one having lost track of days, mistaking Tuesday for Monday. "What should I do?" he said, running his hand through his hair. "Just calm down and sit at my desk and take this exam," I said, handing him a paper then getting up and leaving the office. Grading tests is tedious. Still, occasionally sentences bulge against the grid of blue lines. "Many stories this semester dealt with relations between men and women," a strong-minded girl who wore cowboy boots wrote. "Four stories really caught my attention because each had the men below the women in a way in which I like."

In May I'm too busy to be unhappy. Spring fevers kept me at the doctor's office. Eliza had strep throat then a lung infection. A pitcher hit Edward on the leg at a baseball game. Edward's calf turned into a softball, and he couldn't walk for three days. Athletic doings sprawled across the month. Eliza played on two soccer teams, and Edward, two baseball teams. One day I got up at 4:56 in order to feed Francis then drive him to school so he could go for an early morning run with the crew. The next afternoon I drove to Pataganset Lake in East Lyme to watch him row. Last Saturday Eliza played two soccer games, the first in Glastonbury at 9:30, the second in Marlboro at 2:00.

Children's sports have taught me not to expect success. In the fictional world of tragedy and triumph, teams from small, poor towns defeat teams from affluent, suburban enclaves. Girls from three towns in eastern Connecticut play on Eliza's teams: Willington, Ashford, and Mansfield. Uniforms are simple. Players wear red socks with a black band around the tops, blue or black shorts, and red cotton shirts with the letters *W, A,* and *M* printed in black on the front. Eliza's teams usually win when they play teams wearing similar inexpensive uniforms. Never, however, do her teams defeat squads dressed in "designer" attire. The morning was chilly in Glastonbury, and the "WAM" girls wore a closet of sweat shirts. Except for two sweat shirts with "UCONN" stamped on them, the sweat shirts were different. For her part Eliza wore a sweat shirt with "Sewanee" printed on the front.

In contrast the Glastonbury girls wore shiny customized blue-and-white warm-up jackets. A black and white soccer ball exploded across the back of each jacket, three bolts of golden lightning jagged behind it. Sewn below the ball in bold white letters was the phrase "Glastonbury Lightning State Champions." On the left side of the jacket the player's name appeared in cursive. On the right side appeared the years the girl played on the thirteen-and-under team, 1997 or 1996 followed by 1997, for example. Across the uniforms themselves blue and white stripes sliced diagonally. Printed in red on the shoulders of each uniform was the player's last name. Because a basketball game was taking place at the same time, Glastonbury was forced to play with ten rather than eleven girls. "We'll need at least three extra girls to beat the uniforms," a mother said. The mother was right. Eliza's team lost five to one. After the game Eliza and I bolted a pizza then drove to Marlboro for a twelve-and-under game. The Marlboro girls wore simple uniforms, and Eliza's team won. Throughout the second half a cold drizzle blew across the field. After the game I felt cold. The feeling did not last, though. A boys' game followed that of Eliza's team, and just before we left the field, I heard a father say to his ten-year-old son, "Tyler, give me your coat and take out your earring."

At Glastonbury a father told a story that taught the improbability of an underdog's succeeding. God, the man recounted, was fond of fireworks, and on one July 4, He visited Boston. While God wandered along the dock beside "Old Ironsides," a man recognized Him. The man offered God a hot dog then asked, "how long is a million years?" "To me a million years is the same as a minute," God answered, dumping relish and squirting mustard on the hot dog. "That is interesting," the man said before asking, "How much is a million dollars worth?" "The same as a penny," God said, sipping a Pepsi but wishing for a Coca-Cola. "Well," the man replied, thinking he would trick the Lord out of a bundle, "how about lending me a penny?" "Wait a minute," God said, chewing the last nub of the hot dog.

After one banishes extravagant dream from the mind, pennyworths of ordinary existence please and delight. For four years a friend at the university asked me to take part in a seminar held in Germany. Flying over water frightens me, and I refused the invitations. This year family doings so distracted me that I did not immediately decline the invitation. Shortly thereafter the seminar slipped from mind. By the time I remembered the seminar so many weeks had passed that guilt changed my hard *no* into a soft *yes*. For three weeks before leaving I complained about the trip, at dinner listing athletic events I would miss: three of Edward's baseball games, two of Eliza's soccer games, and Francis's rowing in the New England Championships on Lake Quinsigamond in Worcester, Massachusetts. "Stop complaining," Vicki said one night. "The mole doesn't see what the butterfly is doing. Your expectations are so low the trip is bound to be a success."

Vicki was right. The seminar met near Templin, a small walled city, fifty miles north of Berlin in Brandenburg. East of Templin land dozed into farms. Narrow roads wound between linden trees, crowns of suckers green around their trunks. Storks hunkered atop chimneys, their nests straw hats aged out of blocking. Behind houses red brick barns sank heavy into the ground. Hawthorn bloomed beside walks, and lilacs hung over fences, blue and white then purple, this last smacking of shadowy Persia with its perfumed tea and scented women. From the edges of roads fields of rape rumpled in yellow pillows, hedgerows of tall trees breaking the rolling like creases slicing across smooth blankets. Horse chestnuts bloomed amid the hedgerows. From a distance the cones of white flowers appeared topiary, leaflets cradling the blossoms gently like the hands of gardeners. High above a field a pair of gray herons scissored toward the sea. Lower down two harriers soared and dipped above the rape, yellow seeming to cling like dust to their outer primaries.

Participants in the seminar stayed in a rehabilitation clinic built at the edge of a forest. Laws regulating medical treatment changed just before the clinic opened, and to stay solvent the clinic rented rooms to conferences. Each room contained a television. While I unpacked, I watched the news. Sandwiched between accounts of elections in Iran and France appeared a segment devoted to graduation exercises at a school for strippers. Exposure was thorough, each of the graduates resembling a man fish and during one exercise cradling arms around their bosoms like fullbacks trying to grab balls fumbled in football games.

At practically every hour during the television day I could find people naked and up to something. For a while the rumpusing intrigued me, but then I became interested in more astonishing cavortings, or rather the lack thereof, on what I dubbed "the car program." Throughout the day a car drove across Germany and sundry channels, through villages and farms, down country lanes, stopping and starting at lights and railway crossings. Perched on the seat next to an invisible driver was a camera. A wide lens enabled the camera to photograph the landscape ahead of the car, seeing what a person who never looked to his right or left would notice if he were a passenger. The automobile slipped quietly down roads. In contrast to the throbbing timpani of buttocks and bosom, the silence seemed classical. Participants in the seminar told me that on other programs cameras sat atop boats and trains. One night I floated through a lock in a canal then later chuffed through a tunnel astride an engine. My interest in jauntings on water and rail did not last beyond infatuation, however, and the only transmission that seduced me from the automobile was the aquarium program, not a show, I should add, that would attract the shoals of Carthaginians who attended Hollis Hunnewell's carnival. In Germany the television camera focused on the front of an aquarium, usually one containing gold fish. While fish paddled back and forth, the camera remained motionless. "Viewers," a man told me, "film aquariums and send tapes to the television studio. The program is very popular." "Do people ever make guest appearances?" I asked. "No," the man answered, "just fish. That's enough."

Forty teachers and students attended the seminar, coming to Templin from Germany, Poland, and the Czech Republic. During four days they listened to lectures on and participated in discussions focusing on "The Image of the United States in Literature." The lecturers were American college teachers, two-thirds of whom taught at the University of Connecticut. For my part one night I read from an essay and the next morning led a discussion on "Nature in American Literature." Although many participants were fluent in English, others had difficulty speaking and understanding the language. Few participants knew much about American literature, one man explaining that he was an "expert" on E. L. Doctorow because he found a stack of Doctorow's novels in a bookstore in his village, "the only books in English in the store." Participants had not talked to people with southern accents, and when I arrived, frowns and polite smiles, not words, followed my conversational gambits. Because I addressed participants on the last days of the seminar, I attempted, as another speaker phrased it, to "vaccinate people" with the sound of my voice, eating breakfast, lunch, and dinner with tables of students. Although I worked hard to make myself understood to students, I often missed talks of fellow lecturers. In part I cut talks in order to smooth the hours and exercise myself out of jet lag. I also avoided the lectures because I enjoy natural landscapes more than I do intellectual ones. As I travel years, I rummage the appointments of place. Identifying knickknacks creates the illusion that I belong, if only for a moment. As a result I have rarely experienced the sort of dissociation from time and place that shapes both unhappiness and the successful memoir.

House martins nested under the eaves of the clinic. In the afternoon they looped over fields, cummerbunds of white feathers formal about their rumps, dignifying their wild turns. While wagtails bobbed silently across the lawn, cuckoos sang from the woods, creating their own echoes. The songs of chaffinches rattled through the forest, and blackbirds called from perches high in pines, the melodies fluting and stretching like ribbons of silver water. Supposedly nightingales skulked near the clinic, and after dinner I roamed fields in hopes of hearing a nightingale. I didn't. Still, one evening I saw my first treecreeper, a small brown and white bird that scooted up trunks like a windup toy. At dusk a brown hare trimmed grass growing beside the foundation of the clinic. Mornings and evenings small red deer grazed near the woods. On noticing me, the deer disappeared silently. There being little brush to rustle against or rocks over which to clatter, the deer slipped between trees like shirttails vanishing through doors slightly akimbo.

Like loose chiffon damp green meadows wrinkled through the forest, the trees at grass's edge starched as tulle. Throughout the fields sweet Cicely erupted into constellations of flowers. While stitchwort and forget-me-not blossomed in white and blue clumps, buttercups splattered yellow across the green. Cabbage white butterflies twittered low over the fields, their flights waving and turning like streamers. Holsteins often grazed the meadows, from a distance looking like black and white Dresden figurines. I could not identify several small blue and pink flowers, at times thinking them varieties of cranesbill, speedwell, or willow herb, and as I roamed the woods I planned to return to Germany in order to know Templin better.

On Sunday after the seminar ended I roamed the forest for four hours. Trees resembled those in Connecticut, and I recognized varieties of cherry, poplar, spruce, maple, larch, and white oak. Patches of forest had been lumbered, and cords of wood lay beside trails: birch, beech, and pine. Thick plates of bark resembling medieval armor seemed stapled to the trunks of pine, making the trees appear solid and ancient. As birch aged, dark spread out of triangular fissures and slowly erased white from the bark. All the underbrush, even remnants of logging, had been swept from the forest. As a result stands of beech seemed temples, the smooth trunks columns covered with a green patina. Resembling chips of mosaic, iridescent blue tumblebugs dug into paths between beeches. In seeing beetles as bits of mosaic, I imposed the exotic upon the woods. In fact the forest had been so lumbered and tamed that it resembled a garden, beautiful but not mysterious or threatening. Sweeping undergrowth from the forest struck me as emblematic of man's doings. No matter how man struggles to discipline external nature, no matter the illusion of order he creates, man will never be able to weed his own unruly inner nature. Paths in the woods were broad and flat and often gravel-covered. Almost nowhere in the deep forest did I notice signs of a walker's having strayed from a path.

Much as social institutions direct and restrict thought, so paths, I decided, inhibited individualism, and so "for the hell of it," I forced

myself off paths. Far from gravel I came upon a dead beech. A woodpecker had chopped a hole into the trunk and built a nest, the bird's
droppings whitewashing the bark. Staying off paths tired me, however. I worried that another walker would see then lecture me. Consequently I did not stray from the manicured for long. I should not
have worried about being rebuked, however, for none of the strollers
I met spoke to me, even though I said "good day" in English, French,
and a language sounding vaguely German. "People in East Germany,"
a teacher told me later, "stay on paths. Experience has taught them to
ignore matters that don't concern them."

Eventually I reached a lake and walked toward Templin. Suddenly
I found trash, something that would have made me gloomy in the
United States but which now cheered me. Amid leaves lay a blue
wrapper torn from a stick of Orbit chewing gum, "Winterfresh,"
Wrigleys declared. Stuffed beneath a root was the cardboard top to a
pack of West, "American Blend," "Full Flavor" cigarettes. Only the
narrow and the naive are consistent. When I saw a plastic bottle that
once contained a liter of Coca-Cola, I thought, "America is here. The
beauty of these quiet woods is doomed." Near town appeared beer
cans, signs of the worldwide youth culture, or rather the absence of
culture: Berliner Kindl, Karlsquell Edel-Pils, and Mecklenburger Van
Raven Pilsner, on the front of this last can the face of a knight staring
from behind a beard and the past. Near a road lovers carved initials
into beeches, "F & M" and "WB + GC." Rarely did carvings progress
beyond initials to a heart. On one tree, though, I found the statement
"Pierschel ist Doof," the last word being the equivalent of doofus or
dumbbell.

After spending four days in Germany, I returned home. I left Templin at nine in the morning and flew from Berlin to Frankfurt. After a
five-hour layover I flew on to Boston. At Boston I took a bus to Framingham where I had left the Toyota. The trip took twenty hours. I got
home at eleven Monday night or five Tuesday morning Templin time.
Vicki was waiting for me. "Jesus, you look beat," she said. "Did you
have a good trip?" "I had a wonderful time," I said. "I can't wait to go
back." "Poor you," Vicki said. "Once again you have been deprived of
unhappiness."

Circle

*S*aturday morning was as comfortable as an eiderdown. The day was warm and the sunlight silver. Winter had melted from the mind, and the old lie that living in New England was pleasant seemed true. After breakfast I rode my bicycle around the campus. Blossoms dangled from golden chain trees, wrinkling like yellow curtains. From the sharp buds of umbrella magnolia petals bowed outwards into ladles. On black cherries fingers of white flowers slipped through gloves of green leaves. Fringe trees rinsed the air, and on black tupelos miniature yellow flowers spun sudsy around stalks. Nine blossoms bubbled above one stalk, the flowers so small I used a hand lens to count them. Resembling balls of tissue paper snagged by twigs, blossoms crumpled lumpy over rhododendron. Flats of flowers streamed milky above limbs of double file viburnum, the sterile outer flowers dripping off the flats and hardening into icing.

Waves of lupin rolled across Golf Hill, patches of ox-eyed daisies splashing white through the blue. While sunlight had soiled olive blossoms, staining them pale and sweaty like shirt collars, flowers clustered in yellow knots atop stalks of king devil. Mockingbirds sashayed through scrub. Rarely flying ten feet above the ground, the birds sputtered, seeming irritated by my presence. On the ground starlings bustled through grass, fledglings hurrying after adults, importuning, yet sounding self-important. In front of Gully Hall yellow lilies and purple iris bloomed, the fragrance of the latter provoking dreams in the young. For the middle-aged, however, people who know that life must disappoint, the perfume was too rich. A quilt of clematis draped over a fence, the symmetry of the flowers fearful, almost convincing me that a First Cause stitched the creation together. Scarlet poppies bloomed by the pharmacy building. As buds split, petals wrinkled through seams like evening gowns being forced out of clothes bags.

I rode for two hours. Then I hurried home and drove Eliza to Ashford for a soccer game. Her twelve-and-under girls' squad beat a team from Coventry 9–0. After the game I dug forsythia until Vicki complained that I was shaving the yard. Starting to dig is easy. Stopping is hard. In the morning I'd noticed columbine blooming by the speech building. Because Japanese knotweed had begun to strangle light near the columbine, I decided to move the plants to Francis's garden in the backyard. After wedging rocks out of the ground with a crowbar and filling the holes with compost from the woods, I transplanted the flowers. Because my blood was weedy with energy and the evening was as blue and cool as the columbine, I decided to mow the grass.

While I mowed the backyard, someone walked up the driveway and stole my bicycle from the front of the garage. The year had come full circle. Flowers bloomed, but thieves also budded and blossomed. Last year on the same day, the first Saturday in June, a drug addict cut Francis's bicycle from the rack beside the university bookstore. Before being caught the thief sold the bicycle. On noticing that my bicycle was gone, I jumped into the car and drove around Storrs, a hunk of iron pipe on the seat beside me. "After I get through with the bastard," I thought, "he'll wet himself every time he hears the word *bicycle.*" Fortunately I did not find the thief.

At dinner that night I felt melancholy. Although the bicycle had rusted out of monetary value, I considered it almost an old friend. For twelve years I had ridden the bicycle around Mansfield. Time had broadened the seat, and the bell sounded gritty. Supports for the basket suffered from rickets, and the kickstand had cracked and lost an inch of height. Wrapped around the frame like Band-Aids were stickers advertising Clinton and Gore, the Connecticut Natural History Museum, WHUS, the student-run radio station, and Montgomery Bell Academy, the country day school I attended in the 1950s in Nashville, Tennessee. "Do you think a dope fiend took the bicycle, just like last year?" Edward asked at dinner. "No," I said. "Some kid on a skateboard probably saw it and on a dare ran up the drive, dropped his board in the basket, and raced off. After riding for a while, he probably threw the bike in the bushes and went home." "That's not what happened," Eliza interrupted. "A curator stole the bicycle for a museum. After you die, the museum will show the bicycle. A sign at the exhibit will say, 'Sam Pickering's Bicycle. He rode it while he wrote *Trespassing, Walkabout Year, The Blue Caterpillar,* and other books. The bicycle exerted great influence upon his prose. The brakes were bad, and as a result he rode and wrote carefully. Forced to pedal slowly, he noticed flowers and trees, and they became the spokes of his essays.'" "Don't be so silly, Eliza," Edward said. "She's not being silly," I said. "She is right. Literary historians now own an artifact more important than Mark Twain's house in Hartford." "Or Shakespeare's cottage in Stratford-upon-Avon," Eliza added. "Or George Washington's wooden teeth," Francis said.

Despite the pureed conversation, loss of the bicycle gnawed at me. Last June the theft of Francis's bicycle so bothered us that Vicki and I decided to spend the summer on her farm in Beaver River, Nova Scotia, the first visit we had made in five years. On Monday, two days after my bicycle disappeared, I booked passage for Vicki and me on the ferry sailing from Portland to Yarmouth. During the past year, the farmhouse had been painted, the blueberry field bushwhacked, and the barn roofed. I told friends that we were going to Nova Scotia to check the work. The truth was different. The year had spun through seasons, and the doings of last June had cycled up, awakening association and provoking an automatic, if not thoughtless, reaction. "Do you really want to go to Beaver River?" Vicki asked. "Wanting has nothing to do with buying tickets," I said. "Going to Nova Scotia is something we do in summers, especially after a bicycle is stolen."

As I age, life seems more circular than it did decades ago. Straight lines pointing toward the horizon curve, so much so that the happenings of new years resemble those of old. "Today me, tomorrow you, the day after me again," as Turlow Gutheridge put it, describing repetitive doings in Carthage. In part life appears circular because my mind works by association more now than in the past. Instead of seeing difference, I see similarity. Instead of stirring me to imagine newness, phrases and events now bring the familiar to mind. Not long ago Loppie Groat accused Hink Ruunt of being penurious, saying, "you wouldn't pay a nickel to see a pissant eat a bale of hay." Loppie got things wrong. Niggardliness had nothing to do with Hink's refusal to spend five cents. Hink had aged beyond curiosity. He had roamed the sideshow of life so long that fresh oddities seemed only runners clipped from stale bygones. "Holes in a pond don't last," Hink told Loppie. "No matter the splash a hole vanishes, and once again everything looks like water."

Slubey Garts is an entrepreneurial Christian, and each year in my writings he starts a new business. Last spring he purchased a license for a radio station. Soon afterward WGOD began broadcasting. Along with pushing me toward Nova Scotia, the loss of the bicycle knocked my thoughts into a familiar grove. The day after I bought tickets on the ferry Slubey purchased the Homestead Nursery in Maggart. Although noted for boxwood, the nursery had fallen on dry times. Immediately Slubey changed the name of the nursery to "Watered by the Blood of the Lamb Memorials." Next he hired Isom Legg to clip shrubs into topiary and began a mail-order business, specializing in graveside plantings. Slubey announced "the Christening," as Turlow phrased it, in newspapers published throughout middle Tennessee, the *Carthage Courier*, the *Cookeville Times*, and the *Lebanon Bugle and Trumpet*. Isom owned a hatchery, and among the first topiary advertised were a bird of paradise that looked, Turlow said, remarkably like Isom's prize Wyandotte rooster, Mr. Big, and then a great horned owl which, Proverbs Goforth told customers, would wake at midnight and keep spirits and rats away from the graves of dearly beloveds. The most popular item on the list, however, was "The Rock," a round boxwood planted at the foot of a grave. On Judgment Day, Proverbs informed prospective mourners, the Lord would roll the rocks away and the dead would climb out of the dark valley, "their faces shining like prayer books, no matter that in this life, they'd been uglier than homemade soup."

Slubey's financial successes made less-worldly divines jealous. At the Pilgrim Rest Here Chapel, Mathuzalum Guppy condemned luxury and sumptuous burials, declaring that the only inhabitants of gilded tombs were worms. "Why lay a dead man on a silk cushion when he slept all his life on corn shucks?" The following week Mathuzalum said that only Pentecostals had the right to call themselves Christians. "Folks," he explained, "get above themselves and cover ruined flesh with sticks and leaves. Before they know it, they've become half Christians and have joined the Church of Christ. Next they turn into quarter Christians and Baptists, then Methodists and one-eighth Christians. Finally they become Episcopalians." "If a doctor were to suck a gallon of blood from an Episcopalian, he'd find a pint of whiskey, a jug of country club soda, drippings from water holes on golf courses, but he'd have to parse and splice and endure Hell's own torments before he found a corpuscle of true Christian, much less a drop of right religion."

Slubey rarely responded to criticism. Instead he seized the high aphoristic ground, saying things like "water does not wound" or "the man who sprays black paint on others better dip himself in whitewash." Slubey's assistant and deacon, Proverbs Goforth rarely pulled himself up to the abstract. In Slubey's cause, Proverbs's tongue, Turlow said, was "so sharp that its shadow cut." "I'm not saying Mathuzalum is a snake," Proverbs told the lunch-time crowd at Ankerrow's café, "but if you listen, you can hear scales rattle when he walks." "When the Lord made Mathuzalum," Proverbs told Loppie Groat, "he didn't put any bottom land in the mixings. He used gully dirt and sprinklings of chamber lye." Proverbs even insulted Mathuzalum's wife Zaidee, accusing her of drying dishes with a cat's tail.

Juno Feathers purchased the first topiary Slubey sold. For the grave of her husband Onnie, she ordered a boxwood shaped like one of the Gadarene swine. Not only had Onnie raised hogs, but one evening when he was returning home from Enos Mayfield's Inn in South Carthage, he fell off a bluff and drowned. "When Onnie stuck his snout into sour mash," Juno said, "an unclean spirit got into him. The night he died he ran down a steep place and drowned in the Cumberland, just like those bible pigs what choked in the sea." After Onnie wallowed in the swill, he'd tear the bottom rail off propriety and root up loose boards and smell out grubs and every two-legged carrot in Smith County. One night after spending a long afternoon at the trough, Onnie staggered home and found a canebreak rattler curled on the front stoop. Thinking the snake a sausage, he scooped it up, carried it into the kitchen, slapped it into a skillet, then cooked and ate it. He used the fangs as toothpicks and spat the rattles out, thinking them gristle. When he first tossed the sausage into the pan, it wiggled and hissed, but he reckoned, Onnie said later, "that all the twisting and noise was fat sizzling." If the snake bit Onnie, the bites didn't hurt him. Onnie was so ham-fisted that the venom couldn't reach a vein.

Unlike my accounts of Carthage in which the same silliness goes around and around, in life change occurs and circles break. This year the town sponsored vaccinations for Hepatitis B. Given to children at the middle school, the vaccinations consisted of three shots, the first in January, the second in February, and the last in June, four days after my bicycle vanished. Shots make Francis queasy. After receiving each of the first two shots, he blanched and staggered. I grabbed him and led him to a chair, and Vicki gave him a can of juice to drink. A half hour after sitting down Francis was able to totter outside to the car. This June as Francis waited in line for the last shot, his skin was the color of starch. Vicki and I stood beside him, she with juice in her hand, I ready to seize him if he fainted. Just before Francis got his shot, a girl stepped into line behind him. She was cute and lively and wore a skirt smaller than a napkin. "Francis," she said imploringly, "shots scare me. Will you hold my hand when I get my shot?" Francis did not notice when the nurse stuck him. When he turned toward the girl, his skin was red not white. "Vicki," I said, as she started to hand him the can. He doesn't need juice. His mind and hands are on something else." "Who was the girl?" I asked Francis as we walked out of the school five minutes later. "Maria," Francis said. "She's nice and is in my class at school." "Some things change," I said to Vicki after Francis went to bed. "Maybe," Vicki said. "We'll have to see what next year brings. To me everything seems part of the circle of seasons: winter, spring, summer, boyhood, youth, old age."